Discovering and Embracing

YOUR LIFE PURPOSE

Paul Peters

ELEVATE
PRESS

Bible quotes are taken from the following versions:

English Standard Version® (ESV®). Copyright 2001 by Crossway, a publishing ministry of Good News Publishers. Used by permission.

New International Version® (NIV®).

Copyright 1973, 1978, 1984, 2011 by Biblica, Inc.™. Used by permission.

New King James Version (NKJV). Copyright © 1982 by Thomas Nelson, Inc. Used by permission. All rights reserved.

ISBN: 979-8-9925854-2-1 (ebook)

ISBN: 979-8-9925854-1-4 (paperback)

For more information about Paul Peters and additional resources for *Discovering and Embracing Your Life Purpose,* scan the QR code below.

CONTENTS

PREFACE

The idea for this book came about over many years of pursuing truth and the discovery of principles that I have strived to apply to my own life. As I write this book, wanting to assist others in the discovery of their purpose, I realize that much of who I am will come through these pages. Like you, I am on a quest. I believe that most of us, or at least those who are honest with themselves, are pursuing meaning in their lives. It may be haphazard, but we are all trying to find happiness, joy, peace and some explanation for why we are here. I have provided updated information and tools that I believe will assist readers in narrowing their search.

Although the purpose of this book is to help people discover *their* purpose, I am honest enough to admit that the answer is not always clear. There is never "one way." I will be approaching the subject based on what has worked for me, what I believe provides the clearest path, but I understand many have different beliefs. Although we all share one common similarity—we are all a part of the human race. My writing is not to hinder you, but to give you the tools to help you find your way.

We will go into detail on the pieces of the puzzle that, once put together, will make the picture clearer. The puzzle pieces are various aspects of our journey, like our childhood, our family upbringing, culture, nationality, religion, natural gifts and talents, among other things. My upbringing was based on Judeo-Christian beliefs, so much of what I share about my journey will reflect that background. Also, throughout the book I will be referencing Bible verses and other resources that helped me discover my purpose that I believe will help you as well.

A portion of this book will tell a story of a man named Tim. All names and places in this book have been and will remain fictionalized in order to conceal the identities of the people and places that inspired the events of his story. I will demonstrate through Tim's life how most of us find our purpose, if we ever find it at all.

We will also be looking at other people throughout history who, as we see in hindsight, clearly fulfilled their purpose. I will provide assessments throughout the book to help guide readers. I will provide definitions of terms for clarity.

Thank you for choosing to read this book. My hope is that I will help take you one step closer in the discovery of *you,* and why you are here. These are deep questions that have plagued countless people for countless years. The very act of asking starts the process of discovery. In the search comes the discovery—and in the discovery comes the meaning and fulfillment of one's own life.

INTRODUCTION

Many years ago, a young couple gave birth to a beautiful young boy named Paul. They loved him, and they wondered what role he would play in the world. As they pondered that question, they received a special delivery. It was a letter from God. Never having received this type of letter before, they quickly opened it and began to read. God congratulated them on their newborn son, and laid out for them all that Paul would do throughout his life. God identified his special gifts, talents, passions, personality type, personality style and temperament. All his parents had to do was follow his clear instructions for their son so that his life would have purpose and meaning, and he would be able to accomplish what he had been created to do. The couple then set out to do just that. Knowing this information, they were able to teach, train and guide Paul based on why he had been created and what he was to accomplish. Paul ended up living a complete life that served the purpose for his existence.

"Now when David had served God's purpose in his own generation, he fell asleep and was buried with his ancestors."
–New International Version, Acts 13:36

Wouldn't it be nice if that is how it worked? In some respects, there is truth to this story, as we see in the story of King David referenced in the scripture above. Although in King David's case his purpose wasn't laid out so neatly, and neither is ours. For most of us, this is not how life plays out. In the first chapter, I will share the story of Tim's life, and how he came to discover his purpose. His example is probably more like the lives of the rest of us. My hope is that in his story, you will see that even in pain and struggle, there are answers that can help us discover our purpose. I recently came upon a quote by Mark Twain that best exemplifies my motivation for writing this book: "The two most important days of your life are the day you are born, and the day you find out why."

My hope is that after finishing reading this book you will have discovered why you were created. Another quote that I have recently embraced is "Our story, God's glory." Often our story sets the stage for the revelation of our purpose.

A very wise teacher, Stephen Covey, taught that we are to begin with the end in mind. Unless you can clearly define what you're looking for, how are you going to ever find it? In some respects, I am putting the cart before the horse. Call it a tease, but what we seek, I believe, dwells in the deepest part of who we are. It was placed in us even before we were born. It is a seed, and if we take care of that seed it will grow into what it was destined to be.

As stated in the book of Jeremiah, "Before I formed you in the womb I knew you, before you were born I set you apart; I appointed you as a prophet to the nations." (New International Version, Jeremiah 1:5). This was specific to the prophet, Jeremiah, but why could it not be said of all of us?

My point is that there is something put within us that is meant to meet a need, to fulfill a purpose in our time and in our place in history. This "puzzle piece" gives us the reason for our existence. We are uniquely created for that purpose. My hope is that, after reading this book, you might have a better idea of what that is.

There will never be another "you" in all of time. When all is said and done, and we can look back at our lives in eternity, we will see how and where that puzzle piece fits in the grand scheme of things. The reason I begin with the end in mind is that we have some idea of what we want for our lives.

We get muddled down pursuing the five P's in life: power, prosperity, position, prestige and pleasure. These are easy distractions and even bigger temptations as they always promise more than they deliver. The problem is that we don't realize that until it's too late, and we see the damage caused by those pursuits in the rearview mirror. Often they bring only pain and unfulfillment.

History is littered with examples of those consequences. Civilizations have been destroyed because of these pursuits. If we had the ability to advance ourselves in time, much like in the movie *Click*, using a remote control to see the consequences of our choices, would we be happy? In some respects, we can do this using the creative mind God has given us. We can't necessarily predict our future, but we can set the stage for what it might look like. One of my favorite verses addresses this:

> "For I know the plans I have for you, declares the Lord, plans to prosper you, and not to harm you, plans to give you a hope and a future."
> –New International Version, Jeremiah 29:11

We as humans are finite beings, and God who created us is an infinite being who is not limited to time and space, so he alone can make this claim. When we understand the magnitude of this verse we realize that although we don't know our future, God does, and He desires to bless us. In order to know our purpose we must go to the one who created us, who knows why he created us. He reveals His purpose for us in many ways, and we will examine that throughout this book.

I want to propose, before we dive in, that we stop for a moment and try a couple of things that I hope aren't too radical. First, I'd like you to spend about one or two hours in a cemetery looking at the gravestones. Each has a beginning date and an ending date, but the most revealing part that is left unsaid is the dash between the dates. That is the person's life. Whatever life he or she lived is reduced to a dash. Of course, the memories they left with their friends and family members also reflect that life. Hopefully the person's life left a legacy that speaks of a life lived according to the person's purpose. The second thing I want you to do is to go through recent local obituaries and read some of the comments made by family members of those who have died. Often a paragraph or less is given to define that person's life.

The life we have is ours to live and ours to define. What we do with that life is all we have to give and all that we will be remembered for. It was once said by Socrates that, "the unexamined life is not worth living." Life is more than simple phases: we are born, we play, we work, we die. Life has greater meaning and purpose, and it is up to us to figure that out.

I hold to this belief because I see beauty in all of creation. I find joy in being with those I care about. Life is a balance between yin and yang—good and evil, light and dark, summer and winter. This is what Jesus stated in the book of John:

> "These things I have spoken to you, that in me you may have peace. In the world you will have tribulation; but be of good cheer, I have overcome the world."
> —New King James Version, John 16:33

Knowing that life is meant to be challenging should not be discouraging. As you read Tim's story, you will discover that only out of the pain came hope and direction. This is often how life works. It is one of nature's principles. For a seed to produce, it must break through the soil, enduring rain, wind and drought until it comes to maturity. Often our hardships are part of the journey to discovery. Working through these hardships helps prepare us for what we are to become. Many great men and women became great because they didn't give up when faced with hardship; they allowed it to forge their path to victory and success.

> *"I love those that love me; and those who seek me early and diligently will find me."*
> –Amplified Bible, Proverbs 8:17

This verse references the pursuit of God, but I also believe we must pursue truth. If our desire is strong enough and we seek the answers, they will be revealed, even if it is not in the way we expected; in the book of John, Jesus states that he came to give us life and that it will be a life of abundance.

I am aware of the conflict that arises in all of us. We are first told that we will experience trouble, but also promised that we will overcome the obstacles. We are told that, if we seek, then we will find. Finally, we are told that we are given life, and not just life, but a life of abundance. That lets me know that we have some choices to make.

I remember reading a quote from Stephen Covey that impacted me greatly and gave me a sense of empowerment: "I am not a product of circumstances. I am a product of my decisions." We can't always control what comes at us, but we have a moment—sometimes a millisecond—to decide if those circumstances will dictate our response, or if we will be in charge. It is in that moment that our power lies. We either take it or surrender it. Our decisions define the direction our lives take. My hope is that we will recognize that we have that power in the moment and thus send our lives in the direction of our destiny and purpose.

The third thing I need you to do—and I know I have dragged this out—will be challenging. I want you to write your own epitaph, obituary or eulogy. This should be how you want to be remembered, what you did for others and what you value most. Write what you want your legacy to be. This exercise will provide a visual blueprint of the lives you touched.

I can give you a brief example:

Paul lived his life with a sense of purpose and a desire to serve those in need. He let God and love be his guiding principles. He always sought to be a servant to those in need, and to be a source of encouragement in lifting others up. He always encouraged others to seek God and His purpose for their lives.

These exercises are important references as we go through this book. Not only will they help to define what is important for you, but they will help you draft the purpose, vision, and mission statements we will write later on.

As we delve into Tim's story, we will begin to lay out the tools that will help identify your own uniqueness, and help you realize how special each one of us truly is.

As the psalmist said:

You have searched me, Lord, and you know me. You know when I sit and when I rise; you perceive my thoughts from afar. You discern my going out and my lying down; you are familiar with all my ways. Before a word is on my tongue you, Lord, you know it completely. You hem me in behind and before, and you lay your hand upon me. Such knowledge is too wonderful for me, too lofty for me to attain.

Where can I go from your Spirit? Where can I flee from your presence? If I go up to the heavens, you are there; if I make my bed in the depths, you are there. If I rise on the wings of the dawn, if I settle on the far side of the sea, even there your hand will guide me, your right hand will hold me fast. If I say,

"Surely the darkness will hide me and the light become night around me," even the darkness will not be dark to you; the night will shine like the day, for darkness is as light to you. For you created my inmost being; you knit me together in my mother's womb. I praise you because I am fearfully and wonderfully made; your works are wonderful; I know that full well. My frame was not hidden from you when I was made in the secret place, when I was woven together in the depths of the earth.

Your eyes saw my unformed body; all the days ordained for me were written in your book before one of them came to be. How precious to me are your thoughts, a God! How vast is the sum of them! Were I to count them, they would outnumber the grains of sand—when I awake, I am still with you.

—New International Version, Psalms 139:1-18

Our beliefs dictate our life choices, which dictate our decisions, which affect our emotions and actions that will either positively or negatively impact our lives and the lives of those around us. We have but one life, and our most important choices should be guided by truth, wise counsel and love.

As we venture through this book, we will examine some of the beliefs that affect our decision making and lay the framework for our lives. We will take an honest look at what we believe, and why we believe it. We must be completely transparent with ourselves, as what we believe should be based on personal truth and guided by our own values.

Let me tell you a story. A man asked his wife why she always cut the end of the ham off before she cooked it for a holiday dinner. She replied, "That's how we always did when I was growing up. That's how my mom prepared it." Curious, he called his mother-in-law and asked her why she always cut off the end of the ham. She told him, "That is how my mother always prepared ham." Even more curious, he called his wife's grandmother and asked her the same question. She replied, "Because my oven was too small to hold the entire ham!" My point is that much of what we believe we never question, and we make important life decisions because "that is the way we have always done it."

I end this introduction from a quote from Gandhi:

Your beliefs become your thoughts. Your thoughts become your words. Your words become your actions. Your actions become your habits. Your habits become your values. Your values become your destiny.

Please choose wisely what you believe, because out of that belief will come your destiny. I hope this book will help you find yourself and discover what makes you so "fearfully and wonderfully made" (New International Version, Psalms 139:14). I hope you will begin to learn what you must do to become that "puzzle piece," and to leave your mark on this world, as so many others have done.

CHAPTER 1
TIM'S STORY

TIM WAS BORN IN 1968, THE YOUNGEST OF SIX KIDS IN A RURAL community in southern Illinois. This was at the height of the Civil Rights Movement and the Vietnam War, but of course, as a child, he was oblivious to all of this. He grew up in low-income projects where, from his perspective, he didn't recognize racial differences. He was just another little boy trying to have fun. In fact, his first crush at age four was on a little Black girl whom he referred to as his "chocolate" girlfriend. You see, issues of conflict and hate are not something we are born with; they are a learned behavior. What he saw was a girl whose skin was a different color from his, and from a four-year-old child's perspective, that color most resembled chocolate.

Tim was oblivious to all the drama that was going on at home. Sometime in the 1950s, Tim's mother met his dad in Michigan while she was babysitting his dad's kids from another marriage. They got together, and his dad left his wife to marry his mother. They had six kids in total. First was Sara, born in 1956. Bob was born in 1958. Steve was born in 1959, Joe was born in 1961, Rick was born in 1962. And finally, Tim was born in 1968. His parents struggled throughout much of their marriage.

His dad was an alcoholic, and was physically, verbally and emotionally abusive toward his mother.

Part of what you will see as we venture into Tim's story is how early experiences play a vital role in understanding our purpose in life. Tim's mother would often have to hide from Tim's dad, and hide the kids so they would not be hurt. During this time, they were struggling financially. They couldn't depend on Tim's dad. His mom worked whatever jobs she could get so she could provide for them. Tim didn't grow up with the proverbial silver spoon in his mouth. If anything, they used cheap cutlery handed down from some other family.

After Tim was born, things got much worse. His mom was increasingly frightened by Tim's dad's outburst, threats and violence. Tim's dad was often locked up over domestic violence issues. Tim's mom decided to run away and take the kids with her. Tim's dad found out and tried to kill her. Tim was just a baby at the time. His mom survived and was in the hospital for about six months recuperating. All six kids were divided among the relatives until his mom was well enough to take them back.

Tim's dad was arrested and served time in prison for attempted murder. Tim was later told that his dad came back to see them after being released from prison, but Tim was completely unaware, and hasn't seen him since. Tim's dad lived less than an hour from them when they were growing up and never again tried to reach out. His dad ended up dying alone in a hotel room in 1975 as the result of a heart attack.

So, the first five years of Tim's life were rough. He was raised in an abusive environment and was always afraid. He was raised by his single mom who also had to care for his five siblings while having to work in order to feed everyone. Often these situations lay the groundwork for people's lives and future choices, both conscious and unconscious. Kids are resilient, but to say it didn't have a significant impact would be foolish.

The negative influence of Tim's father did impact Tim's adult life. Once his mom recovered, the family moved from southern Illinois to be closer to her sister in a suburb south of Chicago. She hoped this would provide support for the family, and it was nice to have the whole family together again. Tim's mom worked all the time, so the kids had to fend for themselves with very little supervision.

Kids love to experiment and don't always make the best choices. Tim's siblings had many instances of negative involvement with the law. Tim's indiscretions were much more private as he didn't want to get caught up in legal troubles, but his curiosity led him to drinking, pornography and sexual experimentation—dangerous paths.

Back then, in the late 60s and early 70s, neighbors looked out for each other so the kids couldn't get away with much. If the kids messed up, their moms would find out. If they messed up in school, they were pretty much guaranteed to get two spankings—one at school and another one at home.

Before the move north, Tim's mother met a guy named Bob, who ended up coming to live with them. For many years, Tim thought Bob was his dad, though he found out later Bob was just his mom's boyfriend. Tim respected him but was afraid of him, as he was the one who usually gave him the spankings. Tim knew his mom loved him, and he was happy that she had someone to take care of her and his brothers and sister. He remembered Bob being with them for about three years—and then he was gone.

Tim didn't fully understand at the time what had happened, but he was told that Bob had a heart attack and died. It was weird for Tim. Bob was there one day and gone the next. This devastated Tim's mom, who told Tim later that Bob was the only man she had ever loved, and to lose him at 37 years old really broke her heart.

When Tim was between the ages of five and 10, he either watched TV, (it was sort of like his second mom), or he played outside. Kids can turn almost anything into an adventure. There was a cornfield near his house which was a wonderland of opportunity. He spent endless hours playing hide and seek. He had few friends at that time, and his brothers and sister usually hung out with their friends, not their siblings.

Tim hung out mostly with girls, as they were easier for him to relate to. Little did he know how all these experiences would affect him later in life. Soon after his mom's boyfriend died, his family moved to another town not far from where they had been living, which helped his mom move on.

Growing up, Tim attended several different schools, which was both good and bad. When they left their home after Bob died, he was going into third grade. Tim was a pretty good kid and didn't cause a lot of problems—let's just say he had figured out how to stay out of trouble. After they moved, he didn't have any friends, so he went looking for some.

The kids Tim chose were the troublemakers, the problem kids and the bullies because they were getting the most attention. He remembers being put in a class with the "troubled kids;" the ones who were looking to fight or cause problems. He got his share of spankings from the principal. At nine years old, he was already heading down the wrong path.

Although Tim's mom worked all the time, she was wise enough to get Tim involved in Little League Baseball. He wasn't bad, and the coach took a shine to him. Tim ended up playing multiple positions, like first base and pitcher. While playing on the team, he met a friend whose family was kind enough to invite him on a cross-country trip to California in a Winnebago. It was the memory of a lifetime for Tim. His family could never afford such a trip.

Tim's mom was too busy to ever make it to any of his Little League games. She was working as a waitress at the time, and ended up meeting an older man whom she eventually married. He lived in another town but would stay with them sometimes.

Tim was having nightmares about being on an amusement

park ride like a Ferris wheel. In the dream, he couldn't get off. Tim would wake up scared and screaming. This happened once when his mom's new boyfriend was there. He yelled at Tim, and beat him with a belt. Tim was afraid of him after that night.

One of his memories from that time involved some of the other kids in the neighborhood. They were all smoking cigarettes. One of the cigarettes fell onto the ground and set the grass on fire. Tim immediately ran away. Soon the entire field was on fire. The whole neighborhood came out to help put out the fire while Tim hid under his bed.

Tim wasn't making it easy on his mom. He was getting into trouble: playing spin the bottle, stealing from stores and destroying property. He was supposed to be the good child.

It was around this time that Tim's brother Steve started attending church. Sometimes Tim would go with him; he enjoyed the activities. This was his first real introduction to church, and he became involved in church life. Members of the congregation volunteered at a nursing home facility and conducted church service with the residents. Tim would spend time with them, listening to their stories and singing songs to the residents.

When Tim was in sixth grade, his family moved in with his mom's new husband to the town of Stonewood. This was a good change for Tim—he had been struggling with the direction he was taking, hanging with the wrong kids. Tim's sister had gotten married, as well as his oldest brother. The next oldest had joined the army. Only Joe, Rick and Tim moved with their mom into their stepdad's home. He had three much older kids, as he and Tim's mom were about 13 years apart in age.

He didn't have any friends at his new school and Tim went into his shell. He was in middle school, which is notoriously rough for kids anyway. Back then they called it junior high. Tim was immediately targeted by the other kids and was bullied quite a lot. This was ironic because in his other school, he had been the bully. He ended up befriending another kid who was not a member of the "in-crowd."

Tim stayed out of trouble for the most part, but the bullying continued. There was one kid who would put his foot on Tim's leg while he sat behind him, or he would knock Tim's books off his desk. He and other bullies would all work together to pull Tim off the bus as he was getting on, or pull him away from the urinal while he was using it. Sometimes they would pee on his leg while he was using the urinal. This was very painful and humiliating for Tim, and explains why he and other kids who are bullied have such anger problems.

After a while, Tim had enough. He started standing up to them. He earned their respect and ended up becoming friends with them, though Tim never bullied anyone else again. He had developed a deeper understanding of what it felt like to be bullied. That understanding would eventually play a part in his career choice as a counselor. While in junior high, he was not involved in many activities other than cross-country running. He kept to himself and just tried to survive.

Sometime during junior high, Tim attended a church camp and invited Jesus into his life. He had been attending services off and on, and was involved in some church activities, but he had been more interested in fun than scripture. Before his brother went into the army, Tim went with him to many church functions. He remembers being involved in all-night prayer meetings, though he mostly went to those because they served breakfast in the morning. He would always fall asleep, but he made some great memories.

Home life wasn't great. His mom and stepdad, although married, didn't have the most loving relationship. They drifted apart and mostly lived as roommates. There was a brief period during Tim's junior high and high school days when the family took care of his aging grandmother. Tim had some good times with her, especially playing bridge. But she soon got too sick to care for at home, and they had to put her in a nursing home.

His grandmother stayed in the nursing home for several years. She was diagnosed with cancer, which was very painful for her. Tim's mom told him later how she struggled a lot with her mom. His mom had run away from home when she was in her late teens to avoid her mother, who was very strict. Tim's grandmother raised his mom, her older brother and her younger sister primarily alone. Tim's grandad was known as the town drunk, and his family carried a lot of shame. Tim's mom felt that her mother had taken it out on her.

Near the end of his grandmother's life, Tim knew she and his mom sought to make amends and give each other forgiveness. The entire family was there for her passing, and he believes she and his mom both found peace.

It wasn't long after his grandmother moved into the nursing home that Tim's mom moved into the spare room. He thought this was strange, but he knew his mom and stepdad didn't have a great relationship. Most of the time, Tim would avoid his stepfather, because when Tim did things his stepfather didn't like he would confine Tim to the basement. In some ways, that is what helped to create his vivid imagination. It's amazing the stories Tim could create when he was confined to the basement for hours on end.

As Tim entered high school, he encountered a world that was completely different than junior high. He was attending school with both of his brothers. Rick was a junior when Tim was a freshman, and Joe was a senior. Tim got along best with Joe, who always had a compassionate and caring heart. Rick was a good brother, but he didn't really want Tim hanging out with him. Joe was on the football team, and Tim had always looked up to Joe, so he decided to try out.

His high school days were probably some of the best times Tim can remember, and impacted him considerably in the coming years. He had his first real love, lost his virginity, got his first job and had his first broken bone.

Tim attended a pretty large high school called Howard

Benning High School, home of the Lions. Approximately twenty-five hundred to three thousand students attended the school on two campuses, one for freshmen and sophomores and the other for juniors and seniors.

Tim participated in football all four years. His first two years, he was a wide receiver; his last two years, he played running back. His main competition on the team was his best friend, and they remained best friends for decades.

Tim was always very industrious. If he needed money, his mom always told him he had to work for it. He was earning extra money as early as age six or seven. He would do jobs like mowing grass, shoveling snow, running errands and cleaning houses. When he was in high school, he cleaned the homes of elderly people to make extra money. Tim believes spending time with the elderly, and especially spending time with his grandmother, made a lasting impression on him. He enjoyed their company and really enjoyed talking with them, plus he was pretty good at cleaning. Tim also worked as a paper boy when he was 12 and 13, a time when kids were allowed to have paper routes before the age of 16. He grew up making his own money however he could, but always by serving others. This played a huge part in his career choices, especially as it related to his desire to be self-employed.

The things we do in our childhood build the foundation of who we become, like an unseen hand that guides us to where we need to be. Our future choices can be tracked by the breadcrumbs we have left behind.

In Tim's neighborhood, there was a restaurant he loved called Azarello's. This was the original restaurant in Stonewood, Illinois; it is now a chain with restaurants located all over the United States. He'd always wanted to work there. He went in to apply for a job as a busboy, getting an application from Mrs. Azarello, the owner's wife. She asked Tim how old he was. He said he was 16, the legal age to work. Tim lied; he was only 15. He had gotten pretty good at lying. Tim would later realize that lying was just a defense mechanism that would ultimately catch up with him. Mrs. Azarello believed Tim, and he got the job. He worked there for over five years. The job gave him some of his best memories—it was there that he made some great friends and met his first love.

There he was, going to school, playing football and working. His home life sucked, and Tim tried to stay away as much as possible. His mom was amazing, but she worked a lot, and he hated being at home with his stepdad. None of his siblings really got along with their stepfather, so they tried to avoid him. The holidays were the worst. His stepfather would have too much to drink. His mom would prepare the food, and when they sat down to eat, his stepfather would make a critical comment that would put everyone on edge.

Tim can remember many holidays when his mom went to bed crying because his stepfather had ruined the meal. On one particular holiday, his brother Steve was home from the army. Tim's stepfather was yelling at his mom, and everyone was tense and crying. Steve, a black belt in martial arts, got between his mom and stepfather and told his stepfather that, if he took one more step, he would do whatever he had to do to stop him. Tim thought that would be the end of the marriage, but she stuck by her husband.

The only good memory of his stepfather was when Tim found out his biological father died. Tim's grandmother had hidden this information from the family because she didn't want them to have the death benefits that his father owed his mom. Once Tim's mom received the death benefits, Tim, his brothers, his mother and stepfather flew out to Hawaii to visit his brother Steve and his new wife. Tim was 13. He went cliff diving with his brother Rick.

As he entered his teen years, Tim began to experiment with alcohol. Since he was rarely supervised, he went to a lot of parties. Tim was a people pleaser and had a hard time saying no. He just wanted to fit in and be liked. He often ended up downing large quantities of vodka, gin, whiskey and other hard liquor. He wasn't trying to be rebellious or hurt his parents—he just wanted to be accepted. He was not aware of the damage his actions would cause.

Tim was on a collision course with self-destruction. He experimented with sex and lost his virginity. He was young, and he didn't have a very healthy view of sex or relationships. Like any other young teenager, he was just following his hormones. These early experiences would affect many of Tim's relationship patterns as he entered adulthood.

My point in addressing this is that often we don't always fully understand why we continue to make the same mistakes we always do, or end up choosing to associate with certain types of people. It often goes back to unresolved issues from our past. We are attracted to the type of person who hurt us in the past so that we can fill that emotional void. These attractions are unconscious and destructive, and we end up reliving the pain without ever really healing. As I said early on, be careful what you choose to believe, because that belief will dictate your destiny. When we have unresolved issues due to past trauma, it often sets us up for self-destructive tendencies. In my case, because I struggled with abandonment issues and rejection, I didn't value myself. I felt unlovable the majority of the time, and because of that I never felt worthy. Anytime I wanted a relationship, I would find a way to ruin it. These past traumas have to be healed, or they will keep you in a cycle of self-sabotage.

During those teen years, Tim fell in love with a girl he worked with at the restaurant. She was three years older than him. Her mother, who also worked with them, discouraged them from dating because of the age difference. They dated off and on for about seven years. It was hard for Tim to get over his first love. It eventually ended when he was in his mid-20s due to mutual indiscretions. He was not proud of his choices, and in the end, his heart was broken.

During Tim's senior year in high school, he suffered a broken leg during pregame warmups that ended his football career. He was immediately taken to the hospital where he underwent surgery to install pins to straighten his leg. It was a tragic turn of events for him, because he was good enough to potentially qualify in conference and regional events. That last year of high school was rough, not only because of the injury, but because of the choices he made. His grades suffered, and there was a possibility he might not graduate with his class. He did a lot of makeup coursework and barely passed. He broke up with his girlfriend right after the prom.

I know a lot of this seems like normal teenage stuff, but as you will soon see, our choices have a way of coming back to give us guidance later in life.

Between his low grades and the cast on his leg, Tim was stuck at home the summer after graduation. He pondered what to do. He was still working at the restaurant and loving it. He channeled a lot of his energy into his work. Tim was awarded a scholarship by Mr. Azarello because of his work ethic, and he applied it toward his first year at college. He continued to serve the community, cleaning to make extra money. He loved helping people, but looking back on that time period, he was simply looking for acceptance. Tim was trying to fill that empty hole in his heart—with relationships, alcohol or whatever else worked. Tim got along well with most people, but he struggled to find meaningful connections.

He started classes at the local community college. Unsure what to major in, he decided to take a psychology class. Maybe that would help him figure himself out. He absolutely loved it. One professor had a huge influence on him, though it may not have been the healthiest influence. Let's just say the professor was a free-thinker, and didn't have a traditional Judeo-Christian moral compass. Tim was a sponge, he soaked up everything he learned in his abnormal psychology and human sexuality classes. Tim still remembers his professor bringing in a guy to talk with them about bisexuality. To a young, impressionable, and messed up mind like his, this ended up not being helpful for him. It did set his career choice in motion, although it did detour at times, which we will elaborate on later.

Tim ended up settling into the field of psychology, around the same time that he and his first girlfriend got back together. They had a passionate connection, and though it takes a lot more than that to make a relationship successful, for someone like Tim —who just wanted to be loved—it was perfect.

After his first year at community college, life at home hadn't gotten any better. His stepfather suffered a stroke around this time, and his mom became his caretaker. Tim felt like he had to get away. He started his sophomore year at a junior college near the University of Michigan so he could earn credits to transfer for his junior year. He moved in with his brother at the YMCA. Tim loved the college lifestyle—the drinking, the women, the parties. It was the perfect place for someone on a collision course with self-destruction. Tim was starved for attention. He had no sense of meaning. He was willing to do anything to alleviate the pain he had never really dealt with. He was going to school full-time, working three part-time jobs and doing an internship at the mental health facility, but was only sleeping three or four hours a night. More often than not, he spent his nights drinking himself into unconsciousness. He drank more than seemed humanly possible, and had more sexual relationships than he can remember, sometimes carrying on with three different women at a time. Tim was at a breaking point in his life; he just hadn't realized it yet.

It was Halloween. He was in his third year of college, living with his brother. Tim had invited his best friend to visit for the festivities. Tim dressed up as Rambo and went out to celebrate at one of the University of Michigan block parties. That night, he had an alcohol-induced psychological break. Tim felt indestructible; he was in complete denial of the severity of his condition. As usual, he was drinking. Taking a break from the party, he went into the bathroom and cut his arm with razors. He believed he was Rambo, and wanted to look the part. When he came out of the bathroom covered in blood, his best friend immediately rushed him to the hospital. Tim lied to the nurse and told her he had been in a fight. He didn't want them to send him to the psych ward—he was interning on that unit.

Tim would have liked to say that incident woke him up from all self-destructive behaviors, but it did not. His friend encouraged him to seek help, and finally Tim relented and sought counseling at school. What happened had scared him.

Tim continued to pretend he was okay, and carried on as usual: work, drink and try to numb the pain. This behavior ruined his relationships, and eventually affected his grades. The university suspended him, so he had to take a year-long leave of absence.

Tim went to work with his brother Bob in Chicago doing construction. It was great money, but he was working the graveyard shift remodeling restaurants. He would try to sleep during the day and work at night. Almost every day, the workmen would go out drinking after work and then attend lingerie shows. He wasn't proud of his behavior. When he eventually returned to the University of Michigan, he picked up where he had left off: drinking, partying and messing around.

Tim was not only an alcoholic, but he was involved in multiple relationships with women. He was still trying to find that elusive perfect combination of alcohol and a relationship that would take the pain away. Somehow, he was able to finish college despite his self-destructive tendencies. Tim was burned out in the field of psychology, so he opted to take a job as a restaurant manager. He went through a training program with other new hires, and ended up meeting an amazing woman whom he immediately connected with. She was married, and they started an affair.

Tim had lost sight of his moral compass. In his mind, right and wrong were blurred. Even though he was working a respectable job as a restaurant manager, he was a complete mess.

He was trying to fill his emptiness with sexual relationships. He was drinking like a fish to numb the pain. In his foolishness, Tim quit his steady job to get involved in selling insurance by commission. Yes, it was because of a woman. Unfortunately, this was not Tim's calling in life, and he failed miserably. As a result, he lost both his apartment and his girlfriend.

Tim's life was starting to look like a clip from the movie *Stripes*. His best friend let him stay with him, but that was short-lived—Tim was caught smoking pot and having sex with a woman in his friend's bed. He then totaled his car while driving under the influence. After that, he was not only homeless in a Chicago winter, but also jobless and carless. He snuck into his best friend's basement storage unit to sleep. It wasn't too long before he was discovered and kicked out. He then reached out to a guy he met through the employment training program to see if he could put him up until he could figure something out, but that too was short-lived.

Tim was in his mid-20, homeless, broke and in pain. He could think of only one solution to stop the pain. He decided, as he stared out into the cold water of Lake Michigan, that he was going to drown.

Just as he was entering the water, he heard a clear voice telling him to stop. Tim backed out of the water and started sobbing uncontrollably. He felt God was speaking to him, and made it clear that he was not to throw his life away. Often God allows the pain from our past and our own foolish choices to bring us to a point of surrender so that He can reveal what He has always intended for us. God was going to get Tim through this. So, Tim got himself up and called his brother to finally ask for help.

After his near-death experience, Tim moved in with his brother and his wife and started rebuilding his life. He worked as a waiter on the campus where he had gone to school. He still struggled, but he began to search for answers. He still sought relationships and alcohol but not with the same destructiveness that had once consumed him. He still felt the pull of sex and the lure of temptation; he wanted a healthy relationship, but he wasn't sure how to have one.

Believe it or not, even during this crazy time, he had managed to stay in the military. He joined the army reserves when he was in college, and had found a way to attend the drills. To this day, Tim doesn't know how he did it. The military helped give him some focus. Tim had a strong drive, but it was focused in highly destructive ways.

After much counsel, Tim's brother Joe encouraged him to spend some time in New York with his brother Steve, who was not only in the army, but also a minister. Tim contacted Steve and asked if he could stay with him and his family for a while. He also asked if Steve would mentor and disciple him. Tim didn't fully understand the challenge that this would be—Steve was loving but very strict.

He had been living with Steve and his family for a while when he heard this quote:

"The one who is unwilling to work shall not eat."
–New International Version, Thessalonians 3:10

Tim decided to stop eating until he could find a job. He worked the graveyard shift with disabled adults. Tim absolutely fell in love with them. He didn't realize it at the time, but God was working to reveal Tim's calling. Tim had taken the job only so he could eat, but this job was going to lead him to his life's work.

When Tim moved to New York, he transferred his military status to the National Guard, signing up to be an officer. He was under the tutelage of his brother Steve, who was pastoring a church. During that time period, Tim went away to Officer Candidate School for about six months. When he was there, he was able to focus his energy in a much healthier direction. He worked out three times a day, won the physical fitness award, and was on target to break the candidate award for most pushups, most sit-ups, and fastest two-mile run. He also got to see what he could do as a leader. With his drive, compassion and leadership he was named distinguished graduate of his class.

He also got very serious about his relationship with God and serving others. Tim's life literally did a one-eighty turn. He abstained from alcohol and sex and threw himself into volunteering at the church. He led the children's ministry, helped with the bus ministry and volunteered for visitations. You name it, he was involved. He even joined the choir and sang solos. He met a girl while at church and asked her dad if he could court her.

Tim was a completely different person. Had Tim found all the answers? Not yet, but he was heading in the right direction. For the first time in his life he had a sense of purpose, joy and peace. He had decided to follow God and see if He could help him make better choices. God guided him. Talents in Tim that he didn't know were there started to surface. He began to counsel and minister to his fellow soldiers who were having a tough time, and teach young kids about God. He began to care more for others than himself.

Once Tim got a glimpse of what his potential was and what he believed God could do with him, he knew he would not turn back. Looking back, it was probably one of the best times of his life.

When Tim returned to New York after his training, he got very involved in church and work. He did some volunteering at the local county jail. He attended another church where he took advantage of opportunities to lead the singles ministry and to do some teaching, preaching and speaking around the community. While volunteering at the jail, he ministered to many inmates who struggled with drugs, alcohol and sex addiction. He was even able to lead a class on obtaining freedom from addiction.

It seemed so ironic that God was now using all the pain that Tim had faced to help him help others who were struggling.

Often the very reason God allows us to undergo hardship is so we can develop compassion for others.

Tim finally addressed the root of the pain that led to the self-destructive addictions in his life. He was very involved in the Promise Keepers movement in the 1990s, and attended many of their conferences. He met an inspiring speaker named Dr. Edwin Cole who talked about the need to forgive our earthly fathers. Tim realized much of his pain, emptiness and addiction stemmed from the anger he felt towards his dad for not being there for him. Tim came to realize that his father didn't have the resources he needed to help him through life. This didn't excuse his father, but it helped him understand. When Tim forgave his father, he was able to start healing. It didn't mean that the situation wasn't still painful, but by forgiving his father and letting it go, Tim could find freedom and healing. Tim found guidance in Matthew 5:21–26 (New International Version):

You have heard that it was said to the people long ago, do not murder, and anyone who murders will be subject to judgment. But I tell you that anyone who is angry with his brother will be subject to judgment. Again anyone who says to his brother Raca (hatred or contempt) is answerable to the Sanhedrin, but anyone who says you fool will be in danger of the fire of hell.

Therefore if you are offering your gift at the altar and remember that your brother has something against you, leave your gift there in front of the altar. First go and be reconciled to your brother; then come and offer your gift. Settle matters quickly with your adversary who is taking you to court.

Do it while you are still with him on the way or he may hand you over to the judge, and the judge may hand you over to the officer, and you may be thrown into prison. I tell you the truth, you will not get out until you have paid the last penny.

Dr. Cole, through the words of Jesus, explained that in refusing to forgive his father, Tim willfully allowed himself to be imprisoned by hate. Tim's dad had passed, so he could not physically grant him forgiveness, but he could do so in his heart. Even though his earthly father hadn't been the best example to follow, Tim found comfort in the fact that God, his Heavenly Father, was the perfect model of love and acceptance that he had always needed. That revolutionized Tim's thinking and allowed him to be victorious over his addictions to sex and alcohol. With that victory, he could successfully help others find freedom.

Tim continued to struggle in relationships, as he would often be tempted with women, and he faltered at times as he tried to find "the one." He eventually met a Peruvian woman through work. They ended up getting engaged. She was finishing up school to become a therapist, and they talked about moving to Los Angeles. In the end, they broke up because she refused to honor her obligation to work in New Hampshire for a year. Although Tim was far from a perfect person, honoring your word was valuable to him. This value would later play a big part in his future. The breakup was hard on Tim, but ultimately, he felt he made the right choice.

I am a firm believer that there is an unseen hand—call it God —that guides us to where we need to be. I don't fully understand how even the miserable choices we make still play a part, but they do. It reminds me of the Bible verse where Joseph speaks to his brother about their treatment of him. They sold him into slavery, and after his many years of suffering, he was put into a position of power—second in command of Egypt. With that power, he was able to save his family and an entire civilization.

"You intended to harm me, but God intended it for good to accomplish what is now being done, the saving of many lives."
–New International Version, Genesis 50:20

After that breakup, Tim took a liking to a young lady in the singles ministry. She was beautiful and talented. She had a lovely singing voice. How could it go wrong? Although he had found "the truth," it didn't always factor into every decision. Life is about choices, and learning to use wisdom and discretion in making those choices. Tim, unfortunately, still desired to be loved and accepted. That's all well and good, but success in relationships isn't simply getting those needs met; rather, it's learning how to succeed in a relationship by having the tools necessary to make it work. Tim desperately lacked many of these tools; he had never really seen a healthy relationship modeled as he was growing up. They courted for about a year and eventually married.

In all his years volunteering in the jail, ministering and counseling inmates, he realized he needed to further his religious education. He decided to pursue training at a seminary in Nashville. Given Tim's experience in the jails, he decided to study philosophy to gain a deeper understanding of the Bible and the Christian faith. This came out of many of the questions expressed by the inmates he had faced as a chaplain.

So here he was, recently married, living in Nashville, and working as a groundskeeper at the church where the seminary was located. He and his new wife found a church and got involved in volunteering. As Tim worked and attended school, his wife worked, and they settled into an apartment.

Tim struggled as he tried to deal with issues from his past. His wife felt isolated; her family and friends were up in New York. She found solace in her involvement in the church and eventually worked in missions, joining a mission trip to South America. They were only a little over a year into the marriage when things fell apart. Upon returning from her mission trip, Tim's wife took a job that required her to be gone quite a lot. They weren't talking much or being intimate. Tim began to suspect something was going wrong and had suspicions of an affair. When he confronted her, she left, and his marriage was over. It left Tim devastated. Married just over a year and it was over. The seminary he was attending frowned on divorce, so his career working in ministry was now in jeopardy.

It was a very challenging time for him. He sought counsel from family members, ministers and friends. He did a lot of soul searching. He also made a very wise choice. He decided to make a "life plan." He hired a life coach. They met over a three-day period to look at his whole life and see if there were any patterns that stood out. These patterns could help him identify what his areas of strength and service were. It was revolutionary. Although he felt he had been called to serve in the ministry, he now recognized that he already had been doing that, but in a capacity he hadn't even realized was ministry. He found that his true calling was working with the disabled, and those who were struggling with emotional and psychological issues.

Tim's eyes were opened. Ministry isn't only pastoring a church or mission work; it is serving God in one's area of giftedness. Over the next several years, he threw himself into his work with those struggling with disabilities. He found a new church and got heavily involved in ministry, working with the missions department, the singles ministry and the prayer ministry. During this period, he took a short-term medical mission trip to El Salvador. They went into the mountains and into many of the villages and treated people who needed help. They talked with the people through an interpreter about God and the Bible. They also got to visit some orphanages and the kids who lived there. It was an amazing opportunity to see how others from different parts of the world live. God used that time for Tim to further his discovery of his life's purpose.

Tim had always been an avid reader, so he read voraciously about men and women God had used in the Bible and throughout history to change the world. He was fascinated by the power of prayer to incite change. He read stories about the revivals that had started in America in the 1850s and 1860s and spread throughout Europe. He was especially intrigued with the Welsh revival around the turn of the twentieth century that started out of deep prayer that swept across the nation and dramatically changed people's lives.

He was learning more about his relationship with God as his creator and Father than what he had been taught growing up. Tim's faith was becoming more genuine. He was realizing that alcohol and relationships were only substitutes for real joy and fulfillment. He had the opportunity to go on another mission trip, but this time to an orphanage. He adored kids, even though he didn't have any at the time. He had always wanted to be a father. The main purpose of this mission was to do some repairs at an orphanage and lay a foundation for a new building. It was amazing meeting the kids, who literally had nothing, to see their joy, and to experience their acceptance. Tim felt guilty for never really appreciating all the things he had. It was truly the experience of a lifetime.

Tim's life continued to head in the right direction as he followed God's plan. His purpose continues to unfold, but he has come to recognize that we are not our past, and our past does not dictate who we are to become. Much of what happened to Tim was beyond his control—the actions of his mother, father, siblings, peers and bullies. Often the actions of others, especially the painful experiences, damage us. We may end up with wounded souls, and if the pain is not addressed and healed through love, that wounded soul will seek to heal itself. Without the support of loving family members and friends, we may look for self-destructive ways to heal. We are created with a sense of wholeness of self but this sense of wholeness can be fragmented. It's as if we are trying to find all the pieces that make us "us," and put them back together so we feel whole again. God can help to heal that wounded self, to find all the broken pieces and put them back together.

Has Tim "arrived?" Not completely, but he is on his way. Although not everything was clear from the beginning, in his discovery of his calling, he has learned. God gave him clues. On that dreaded night when Tim was at the end of the rope and wanted to throw his life away, God intervened. God knew his future, and if Tim had killed himself, many lives would have suffered. Tim would never have fulfilled God's purpose. Because Tim did listen, God began to reveal to Tim in every experience—good and bad—that "in all things God works for the good of those who love him" (New International Version, Romans 8:28).

As I reflect on Tim's story, I also reflect on what God has taught—and continues to teach—me. I would like to share a little of my own story. Like Tim, I too became involved in mission work. On one trip, I became close friends with one of my teammates, and upon our return, began to spend more time together. She worked at the church in the audio/video department and sang in the choir. We ended up dating. We courted, did everything right and abstained from sex. It was wonderful to experience a relationship that was done right. She had a 10-year-old daughter, and we all got along great. After courting for a year, we got engaged, planning for an April wedding.

Prior to our meeting, I had been working as a group home manager at a residence that served folks with developmental disabilities. I loved working there, and each of the residents participated in the wedding as ushers. They all got to wear tuxedos.

I switched positions prior to our marriage and went to work for an area program as a case manager overseeing services provided for folks with developmental disabilities. After the wedding, we settled into a home in North Carolina that was built around the time Lincoln was president. My wife had lived there for several years. We had our first child, Reece, in 2001. Our second child, Elliot, was born in 2002. Reece's first name is Paul, and Elliot's first name is Paige. We named Paul "Reece" after the famous revivalist Rees Howell, whose passion for prayer had a huge impact on me. We named Paige "Elliot" after Elizabeth Elliot, a missionary who lost her husband to cannibalism. Their love story played a big part in our courtship.

When our third child Jordan arrived, we moved into a larger

home in Charlotte, North Carolina. I took a new position working for a company in Albemarle managing a sheltered workshop that served individuals with disabilities. I also worked helping individuals with disabilities start their own businesses, as well as overseeing a transformation of the Intermediate Care Facility program. I wrote and received grants that helped bring in a sensory room to help those with behavioral challenges. It was an opportunity to make some real and lasting changes in the community.

Around this time we also started working with the foster care system. We decided to open our home to those with developmental disabilities. The first young lady we welcomed was permanently disabled as the result of a brain tumor. She had lost most of her ability to care for herself. She was in her early 20s, and had previously been living with her grandmother. We cared for her for about two years until she passed away. We eventually moved to a larger home in the neighborhood, and we took in another young lady.

We were both very active in the church. My wife sang in the choir, and we both taught classes on finance. Our church was very open to having people teach classes, as they had a very active teaching ministry. I was able to teach a course called "Experiencing God." I also created a course called Finding the Purpose of Your Life.

That was the beginning for me and my research to help people understand what they are supposed to do with their lives. I was meeting so many who were unhappy in their work, so mismatched with what they were doing. I didn't see any formal training available to help people figure out what they were created for. That is why I created the course, and why I sought to teach others what I had learned. I have sat on this project for ten years, and finally decided to put it into a book.

Life was going well, but it was very challenging. My wife stayed home with the kids while I worked. I left the job in Albemarle and took another job in Charlotte doing case management.

When our kids were around four or five, our marriage started to suffer. The stress of raising kids, working, and caring for individuals with disabilities in our home took its toll. Our communication and intimacy were affected, and I was struggling with how to address conflict. I have never been one who handles conflict well; I tend to isolate and withdraw. I decided to meet my needs in ways that were not healthy. I turned to the internet to look at things that were not healthy or conducive to a good relationship. When my wife discovered this, she nearly ended our marriage.

I sought forgiveness, and did everything possible to try to address our problems through counseling, support groups and taking accountability over the next year, but to no avail.

Early 2008 marked the beginning of a three-year long battle for my kids that changed everything. I wanted to fight to be a part of their life, since my Dad was not part of mine. It cost thousands of dollars. I could only see my kids during the first six months under supervision because of things that were said about me. My children were removed from my home and medically examined based on those allegations.

I fought like hell to reveal the truth and to regain my children. I was eventually cleared of all charges, and granted joint custody in 2011. During that difficult time, I took every opportunity to spend as much time with my kids as I was allowed. Because of that, I was able to maintain a good relationship with them, despite what was said about me. I've maintained that relationship to this day.

Through all of this, the biggest impact besides the end of my marriage was the number of friends I lost. After the discovery of what I had been looking at on the computer, I submitted myself to the leadership of the church for help. Once the accusations were made, the support from the church and my friends was suddenly gone. It took me years to get over my abandonment by my church. I almost never wanted to attend church again. The silver lining was that it forced me to examine what church was and what it wasn't. For me, it isn't a building, and it isn't just a place where people come together. It is more like a spiritual hospital where people come to find acceptance and to be healed.

I share this with you to demonstrate that, even when we try to do things right, life can throw us some curveballs. People will betray us and let us down. This is all part of God's plan. Was I wrong to have been looking at something I shouldn't have? Yes. But did I continue? No. And did I seek help? Yes. Did it make a difference in saving my marriage? No! Did it make a difference in me, and motivate me to seek forgiveness and healing? Yes! Was I treated fairly for indiscretions? I don't think so, but life is not fair, and to quote a friend, "It is time to put your big-girl panties on!" (but in my case, it was big-boy boxers).

After our separation, I was in survival mode for a long time, just taking things day-by-day. My whole life had been ripped from me, and the things that mattered most were gone. But if nothing else, I am a survivor; it's one of the qualities I got from my mom. If I didn't have my kids to fight for, I can't say I would have had the same resolve. I was severely hurt, but not done!

I had the opportunity to do what my father hadn't done, and I was going to do whatever it took to get my kids back. They were able to say that their dad never quit fighting for them. The things I learned, although painful, far outweighed the negative experiences.

I threw myself into my work as a coping mechanism. I was given the opportunity to start a company with an acquaintance. The state was allowing private providers to enter the network to service those with disabilities. Our company grew. I was excited, but was beginning to have some ethical concerns. One of my strengths—or weaknesses, however you want to view it—is that I am very trusting, and I always try to see the best in others. In this case, I trusted the wrong people in my company, and as a result, I was forced out of business. This turned out to be a godsend, as the state started allowing providers in the network to do case management services. I applied and was accepted. Covenant Case Management Services was born in 2010.

Although I wasn't attending church, I didn't blame God for the choices of some of His followers. My relationship with Him remained strong. My company grew quickly. I took on additional staff in 2014. Now we have close to two hundred staff members with locations in twenty-eight counties. We went from income of $1 in 2010 to over $5,000,000 in 2019.

When the state took over managed care, we had to complete an application to be considered a community guide agency. As an advocate, I went up to Raleigh fully aware that the bill that had been placed into law did not allow managed care organizations to do a request for proposal. The law clearly stated that all private case management agencies would transition into the network providing community guide services. I completed the request for proposal and submitted it to the managed care organization (MCO) in Mecklenburg to discover Covenant had not been chosen. I hired an attorney, who submitted a letter to the MCOs informing them that, if they did not comply with the law and allow Covenant and the other agencies who were previously providing case management services into the network, then further legal action would be taken. Shortly after that, Covenant was awarded a contract with both MCOs to provide community guide services.

It is important, in the context of understanding our purpose, how events in our lives, especially the ones we can't control, help to guide us. Despite these challenging times, I have devoted a lot of my time and effort to be with my kids. My intense love for my kids made me conquer my fear of confrontation and my people-pleasing tendencies. I learned to fight for what I believed in. That soon carried over into my career as I fought for causes that were worth fighting for, no matter the consequences. I recognized that it is not so much the event that defines us, but how we respond to that event.

After the separation from my wife and children, I had the opportunity to take in a young boy who was diagnosed with special needs. This was an unusual case, as he was being taken care of by a family member at the time, and he himself had a tough childhood. That child was my saving grace during this trying time. Oftentimes, God sends us people we can minister to who also minister to us. I have had the honor and privilege of caring for this young man for 13 years now, and I consider him my son. After three years of custody proceedings, which culminated in joint custody, I was a single dad raising a seven-year-old girl, an eight-year-old boy and an 11 year-old boy with special needs. Challenging, yes, but I loved it. Over the years, many individuals with disabilities have lived in my home, and I have cared for them as if they were my own. I made that choice because it became clear to me that it was my calling, and I was faithful to that calling. The loss I experienced as a young man who grew up without a father has helped me to be the "Father" for others.

When we commit to the obedience of the doing, the reward follows, which is peace, joy, fulfillment and love! As my kids have gotten older. I have tried to be true to my purpose in their lives. I have a message posted in my kitchen, and I read it every day to remind myself of my responsibility as a steward to my kids. It goes like this:

I am a good and loving father who lives out his passion and purpose to wisely teach, counsel, love, laugh with, serve and enjoy my kids.

As I have sought to better understand God's role for me and have Him reveal to me my calling, that purpose continues to unfold. Years ago when I made that life plan, it revealed the previously unseen hand of God working in my life to steer me towards working with the disabled. As I have done that for almost 30 years, He is now bringing back something He started in my heart almost 15 years ago—helping others find their purpose in life.

Covenant Case Management Services is God's company. We have grown from serving one family in 2010 to serving almost four hundred in 2019. We can now minister to so many. I am humbled by what He has done. God gave me a vision 10 years ago of what He wanted. I have tried to be faithful to that vision, and it has now become a reality.

As I said before, God knows what we are to do and be, even before we are born. He has an intention, and if we look to Him, He will show it to us. If we listen and obey, He will fulfill His purpose in our lives—why we were created. God has blessed Covenant and the families we serve. He has helped me to bring in employees who work with similar hearts and passions as mine. I am working on directing others to seek Him. I want to help them identify their gifts, talents, strengths and passions, and put them to work where they will use these gifts to thrive and prosper.

If I am doing something I love and am called to do, I am successful, and this has taken me down another path. Given my disillusionment with the church, I chose to use that experience, not in criticism or condemnation, but in service. I formed a nonprofit group known as The Nehemiah Project Covenant of Love. This idea came out of much prayer and study in the Book of Nehemiah.

To summarize the story, Nehemiah, a Jew, was cupbearer to King Artaxerxes of Persia around 444 BC. His home city of Jerusalem was in ruin after the destruction of the wall by their enemies. The Jews had just been released from captivity, and Nehemiah was sorrowful over the condition of his home. His master saw his sorrow and asked how could help. He asked that he be allowed to return and assist in rebuilding the wall and help restore the city. The king allowed this and paid for the venture. Through much difficulty from their enemies, Nehemiah and the other Jews restored the wall and the city to its former glory.

There were seven towers in Jerusalem that had to be restored. God revealed to me the symbolic significance of this story given the current condition of our modern cities. He helped me to see that each tower represents an area of our society that is broken and needs to be healed: seniors, veterans, those struggling with addiction, the intellectually and physically disabled, those suffering with mental health issues, the homeless, and abused mothers with at-risk kids. This past year, The Nehemiah Project began serving these towers first in Stanly County, North Carolina, and ultimately throughout the whole state:

Our Mission: To meet the needs of those in our community who suffer and are hurting. We do this by loving, supporting, mentoring and serving in order to give hope and a sense of purpose within their community.

Our Vision: To see our community coming together in love and unity through acts of service toward one another that will restore and bring healing to rebuild our community.

Our Purpose: To rebuild, restore and bring healing to our community by uniting together and serving one another in a spirit of love, kindness and compassion.

Rather than solely working directly with the church, we have chosen to work with the church and other community partners that have a heart for those in each of the towers. In this way, we come together to help restore the community, just as Nehemiah did in his time. This sort of effort starts with a heart's desire to serve and minister, and is followed by a sorrowful heart that wants to do something about it. It requires an obedient heart to go and do the work. Most importantly, a humbled heart is necessary to allow God to help in the process.

Recently, I have been given the opportunity to have my own TV show called *On Purpose with Paul* (which can be seen by visiting *nowmedia.tv/on-purpose*). It allows me to not only tell my story, but allows others to tell their story of how they are discovering God's purpose in their life.

In this chapter, I have sought to share Tim's story as well as some of my own. In the pages that follow, I intend to give you the tools you can use to begin discovering what your calling is. The tools will help you find your strengths, your passions, your temperament or bent, your spiritual gifts, your personality type, your personality style and your overall experience. Together, these attributes will all come together to make you the amazing person God intended you to be.

CHAPTER 2
WHY ARE WE HERE?

PEOPLE HAVE WONDERED ABOUT THE MEANING OF OUR EXISTENCE for as long as we have been alive. Since everything else created has a purpose, then why not humans? A hammer was created for the purpose of pounding things. An apple tree was created to produce fruit. A cow was created to produce milk.

Depending on what we believe regarding the origin of the human race, the answers will vary. I will not use this chapter to debate the theories related to evolution versus creationism, but knowing that we ourselves are creators, it seems reasonable to believe we were also created. If we were not created, how can we have a sense of purpose or meaning for our lives? There must have been some intelligent designer behind the scenes with a plan. So, for the sake of consistency, let's assume we were created. I will not get into the much debated issue of man's origin, only to say that it makes sense that whoever created us had a purpose in mind to meet some need in the world.

"Know thyself" is an ancient Greek aphorism. If we are to best understand the purpose of something, we must first study it. For example, in order for me to properly use a power circular saw, I must understand how it works. It is always best to read the instruction manual to ensure I know how to set it up and how to use it safely. If I follow the instructions, it's reasonable to assume I should be able to use it successfully.

Although we are not power tools, we are created beings, and I believe we too come with an instruction manual. It is called the Bible, and if we properly follow these instructions, we can know ourselves—all of the parts, our Creator's purpose in creating us, and what we are to do in our lives to fulfill that purpose. We also have something useful inside of us—our intuition. Some people are more gifted at following their intuition than others. Your intuition is your inner "knowing." One of my favorite verses is from Romans:

> *Therefore, I urge you, brothers and sisters, in view of God's mercy, to offer your bodies as a living sacrifice, holy and pleasing to God—this is your true and proper worship. Do not conform to the pattern of this world, but be transformed by the renewing of your mind. Then you will be able to test and approve what God's will is—his good, pleasing and perfect will.*
> –New International Version, Romans 12:1, 2

This has everything to do with surrendering to "the higher purpose." Deepak Chopra refers to this as the "law of detachment," or letting go of the outcome. When we surrender, the outcome will show up as it was meant to. This applies to relationships, money and everything else we encounter in life.

Humans are probably the only creatures that have been created who are not innately aware of their built-in purpose. Why is that, I wonder? Allow me to theorize for a moment. Referencing the original creation story, I believe Adam and Eve did at first have that innate sense of purpose (Genesis 1:28, NIV):

> *God blessed them and said to them, "Be fruitful, and increase in number, fill the earth and subdue it. Rule over the fish in the sea and the birds in the sky and over every living creature that moves on the ground."*

They knew they had been created to have an intimate relationship with God and to care for the things He made for them. When they disobeyed that intimate relationship with God, their sense of purpose was hidden from them.

We would not ask questions about the meaning of our existence if we didn't believe there was one. I believe God created us for a relationship with Him, and to worship Him. According to the Bible, when we seek Him, we will find Him. In finding Him, we find our sense of purpose. Fortunately, God is much wiser than we are, and He knows us better than we know ourselves. He knows the great gift He has instilled in each of us. That doesn't mean he makes it easy. I've learned that anything that comes easy is not worthy of knowing, because it will not be appreciated. God requires us to commit ourselves to knowing Him and seeking to know ourselves more than anything else. As is said in one of my favorite passages:

> Jesus replied, "Love the Lord your God with all your heart, And with all your soul, and with all your mind. This is the first and greatest commandment. And the second is like it: Love your neighbor as yourself."
> –New International Version, Matthew 22:37–39

When we love Him with all that we are, and we love others as we love ourselves, God will reveal His purpose for our lives. Our purpose in life is directly related to the capacity to love and serve one another, based on what gifts, talents and passions God has given us. Why are we here? Simply to fulfill God's purpose:

> "Now when David had served God's purpose in His own generation, he fell asleep, he was buried with his ancestors, and his body decayed."
> –New International Version, Acts 13:36

Jesus is the perfect example—he not only knew why he had been created, but he knew what he was supposed to do each and every day, even if that meant surrendering to his enemies to be killed. His sacrifice was his ultimate purpose. Jesus had total communion with God the Father:

> *"For I did not speak on my own, but the Father who sent me commanded me to say all that I have spoken."*
> —New International Version, John 12:49

Also:

> *"Jesus gave them this answer, 'Very truly I tell you, the Son can do nothing by himself; he can only do what he sees his father is doing, because whatever the Father does the Son also does.'"*
> —New International Version, John 5:19

We don't have the ability to know the future, but wouldn't it be nice to be prepared for whatever happens? In some respects, we can be. I am a firm believer that God knows all past, present and future simultaneously, since He exists outside of time. He knows what tomorrow looks like, and if I follow that logic, I recognize that He is a loving God and He wants to help prepare us for what's to come.

CHAPTER 3

WHAT IS "PURPOSE" AND HOW DOES IT RELATE TO US?

I WOULD LIKE TO START THIS OFF WITH A QUOTE FROM SECOND-century philosopher, Patanjali:

> When you are inspired by some great purpose, some extraordinary project, all your thoughts break their bonds, your mind transcends limitations, your consciousness expands in every direction, and you find yourself in a new, great and wonderful world. Dormant forces, faculties, and talents become alive, and you discover yourself to be a great person by far than you ever dreamed yourself to be.

Purpose gives us meaning in our lives. It fuels our passion for what we love and motivates us to serve others. Too often we fail to find purpose because we look outside of ourselves to find it. We look for it by comparing ourselves to others, or by wanting to win the approval of others.

I believe God allows challenges to make us stronger. Working out with weights is a good example. If a person wants to look buff, he or she must exercise. The simple process of weight training tears muscles down in order to build them up. If a person is disciplined, they will achieve their fitness goals.

It is no different when you are pursuing your purpose. To use another practical example, as I mentioned, I liken purpose to your inner GPS. Once you know your purpose then you set your destination and follow the instructions to get where you want to go. Unfortunately, many people don't know their destination, so they struggle with taking that first step. To use a quote from German philosopher Frederick Nietzsche, "When you know your why, you can endure any how."

Holocaust survivor Dr. Victor Frankl wrote a book called *Man's Search for Meaning* after his horrific experience in a German concentration camp. He sought the reason that he and others survived, when all of his friends and family members had perished. He firmly held onto a belief that his life had meaning and purpose, and that is what kept him going. His sense of purpose came out of the crucible of his suffering, and the world is forever blessed as a result.

History is full of examples of men and women who surrendered their lives to their higher purpose or mission. While serving as a nun in Calcutta, Mother Teresa ministered to the poor and dying. Everyone who knows about her can clearly say she lived out her calling—her purpose—in life. Her sacrifice is inspiring, but when we discover our own purpose and commit to it fully, there is no sacrifice. Serving the poor brought Mother Teresa incredible joy.

Martin Luther King Jr. was a minister by profession, and born at a time when the world needed him. He was faithful to God's calling to be a voice for the oppressed. He, too, sacrificed both physically and mentally for his purpose. Because he did, the country took a huge step towards racial equality.

It's easy to say, "Well, I'm no Mother Teresa or MLK Jr." But you know they probably said the same sort of thing at some point in their lives. We are not put here to be great; we are put here to find our purpose and serve others, and though we should never pursue it, sometimes greatness is the reward.

True greatness shouldn't be measured in the accolades we get from others or the accumulation of wealth, but in the value of our service to others. Mother Teresa was not pursuing material wealth or fame. She simply had compassion and a desire to serve her fellow humans. There are many who are truly living out their purpose, and I consider them my heroes. Tony Robbins and Jack Canfield have achieved accolades and wealth, but that was only after they had worked their butts off, discovered their purpose, and served others by helping them to become the best versions of themselves.

The key to success is recognizing that your main goal in life is to be the best "you" you can be. That doesn't mean it is all about you, but if we are truly to love others and serve them, then we must love ourselves first. This is fueled by the ultimate love, which comes from our Creator. If you believe that God doesn't make junk, then we are forced to love ourselves.

As we examine some of the tools you will use to discover your purpose, many of us will be forced to heal old wounds. We can't settle for what our dad or mom or anyone else may have said about us. We often allow hurtful words to define us. We find ourselves far from God's original purpose because we were led off the path by an unhealthy caregiver who was hurt or damaged. The importance of healing yourself and finding your identity is vital in your pursuit of purpose.

For me personally, I began to grow when I stopped blaming what had happened to me. I recognized that, as much as my mom and others loved me, they had their own issues. They were doing the best they could. Whatever I was going to believe about myself had to line up with the truth. I learned a long time ago that my feelings were not always the most reliable indicators of truth. I also recognized that many of these feelings were simply projections of my innermost fears.

As a Christian, I had a choice to make. I was either going to believe what God was saying or I wasn't. I tried to look at it rationally, logically and emotionally. I took into consideration all that God had done for me, first in creating me with a sense of purpose, and also saving me from my self-destructive choices in life. He set me on a path of self-discovery by enabling me to discover who He was.

I simply decided that, if God had created me, He must have had a reason. My responsibility was to find that reason. This book is about that discovery. When we discover the why, we can endure the how. I believe God will reveal all things to us. When the student is ready, the teacher will appear.

CHAPTER 4
THE SEARCH FOR ANSWERS

As I said before, I believe we are all born with certain gifts and talents. I liken them to Christmas or birthday presents that haven't been opened yet. Searching for the answers is like opening the present and discovering what's inside. In life, it's not that quick or easy. We are also given a certain temperament and personality. If we develop our gifts, they can become tools that lead us to the answers.

No two people are the same—even twins. Often when we are born, we may be labeled a good baby or a whiny one based on our behavior. Opinions like that can reinforce our own beliefs about ourselves—beliefs that may or may not be true. We want to please our primary caregivers in order to receive the love and attention we need. Some children are quicker at communication or mobility. Some kids have natural talents for art, music or sports. Some kids may not display their innate gifts right away. Sometimes those natural gifts are indicators of our purpose. They should be considered as we evaluate the other elements that we will address in this book.

There are various aptitude assessments that can help us identify our natural abilities. Historical figures like Michelangelo and Leonardo da Vinci had an aptitude for art, while Mozart and

Bach had an aptitude for music. When those natural gifts are discovered, they should be pursued if they bring the person joy. Sometimes people will turn from their natural gifts if they are exploited or pushed too hard. As a result, they are never able to use their gift to the fullest potential.

This is addressed in Proverbs:

> *"Train up a child in the way they should go and when he is old, he will not depart from it."*
> —English Standard Version, Proverbs 22:6

We as parents may see a natural gift in our child, and should encourage that. But a child should never be pushed too hard, or it can create a misalignment from their purpose. In my book *Success Redefined*, I shared the four elements of success. I discuss the importance of having a vision, a sense of purpose, to be fueled by passion and driven by love. Those four elements will bring you success.

One of the keys to understanding your purpose, if you have natural aptitude, is nurturing a passion and desire to use your gift. Michelangelo and Leonardo da Vinci were not only talented; they were passionate about what they did. Speaking about his sculpture of an angel, he said, "I saw the angel in the marble and carved until I set him free."

Often the belief is that success is found in those who have high intelligence, but as it pertains to purpose, that is not always the case. Although intelligence sometimes plays a role, it is not the only factor. Both Einstein and Edison had minimal formal education. Edison only attended school for four months, and then was taught by his mother. Einstein's instructors believed he had learning disabilities. They predicted he wouldn't amount to much intellectually. Both men are known geniuses. Although they excelled intellectually, they set their marks in their fields more for their senses of purpose, curiosity and passion.

When we seek answers, God gives us clues. In the last year, God has given me my own puzzle pieces to help guide me in my endeavors to help others. These puzzle pieces bring me closer to the finished picture. For example, God led me to the book of Nehemiah. As I read the story of Nehemiah rebuilding the city, God led me to name my nonprofit The Nehemiah Project Covenant of Love. We find the phrase "covenant of love" in Nehemiah 1:5. He revealed that each of the seven towers represented a great need in each community that was in disrepair: seniors, veterans, those struggling with addiction, the intellectually and physically disabled, those suffering with mental health issues, the homeless and abused mothers with their at-risk kids. Just as Nehemiah worked side-by-side with the Israelites to rebuild the wall, the Nehemiah Project brings people together to rebuild their communities.

Once God's great vision was revealed, I prayed for guidance.

Several years ago, a friend invited me to her church in Albemarle. She had asked me several times, but I'd been unable to attend due to scheduling conflicts. One particular Sunday, I felt compelled to go, so I ventured to church only to find that she wasn't even there. Instead, they had a guest speaker, Pastor Larry. I wept as I listened to him speak about his ministry—working with men who struggled with addiction. This subject was close to my heart, as I had gone through similar struggles many years ago.

The next day, I told the story of Pastor Larry's profound impact on me with my team in our prayer meeting. One of my friend's jaws dropped open. She said that Pastor Larry had played a major part in her life during a time of difficulty, and was now a good friend. Later that week, the friend's mother shared information with us about an upcoming meeting of community members who were interested in helping those that were struggling with addiction. A few of us attended. As we sat in the front row, I leaned over to her and said, "Your friend Pastor Larry should be here." She texted him, and while she was typing, she looked up and discovered that he was sitting behind us! I met him briefly after the meeting and told him we should grab lunch.

When we shared our stories, we realized we had the same heart for serving. I got involved with some of the men he was ministering, and eventually started attending his church. Long story short, God was leading us to start our service in the area of addiction. The clues He left had made it clear.

I met Larry's wife, brother and sister-in-law, all of whom attend the same church. God revealed to me that I should bring their wives on board with us at Covenant. He later made it clear that they should be the directors of the Nehemiah Project. Both women had servants' hearts and had partnered with many other community groups. We were beginning to bring about God's vision.

God then opened up doors for us to begin ministering at-risk kids in Albemarle. We reached out to some of the schools about allowing us to spend time with the kids during lunch. We wanted to build trust with them, and that connection has allowed us to help many of the kids and their families with their housing, transportation and employment needs.

God has often brought people and supplies in our path that happened to meet the very needs of those we were serving. It's exciting watching His vision being lived out each and every day. God gives us the blueprint, and our action brings that blueprint to life. God is the architect drawing up the plans. He guides us by giving us those puzzle pieces along the way. As long as we continue to seek those answers, the picture of the finished product becomes clearer. The key is to take that puzzle piece and place it down where it goes, and then put the next one down where it goes. When we trust Him, our path will be clear.

CHAPTER 5
HOW DOES LIFE EXPERIENCE AFFECT WHO WE ARE AND WHO WE BECOME?

IN WAYS THAT ARE NOT ALWAYS CLEAR TO US, OUR LIFE EXPERIENCES directly impact who we become. Even though, to a great extent, we control the choices we make, there are forces within us that steer us away from good choices.

I have learned a tremendous amount from my work with those who live with disabilities. A disability—physical, mental or emotional—does not define a person, just as a person is not defined solely by their profession. There are countless stories of successful men and women who were either born with a disability or were later encumbered with one. I am not denying that the disability may cause some challenges, but they can also bring opportunities.

One of the greatest gifts God gave us is the power of choice. Even when bad things happen, we have a choice in how we respond. Our belief systems and attitudes play a vital role in our outlook on life. Many people who have suffered untold tragedy did not allow themselves to play the victim and place blame. All that does is leave us powerless to change. Instead, they took it as an opportunity. Although God does not desire evil to be done to us, He can use what has happened to help us grow.

One of the greatest historical illustrations of this concept is found in Genesis 37-50. Joseph was the son of Isaac, and was gifted with the ability to interpret dreams. He was Isaac's favorite, the firstborn of his beloved wife Rachel. Joseph's brothers were jealous. They hated Joseph, and sought to kill him, but decided instead to sell him into slavery. They told their father he had been killed. For many years, Joseph was a slave; he was falsely accused and imprisoned. But God continued to watch over him, and Joseph found favor with his masters. After many years, he was released, and due to his skill and wisdom put in a high position, second-in-command to the Pharaoh of Egypt. Once in command, he had the option to take revenge on his brothers, but he did not. He knew that what they intended for evil, God had meant for good. God could save the Jews from famine under Joseph's leadership. None of that would have been possible had his brothers not done what they did.

So in the midst of our suffering, we may not know the end result. But if we are obedient and sensitive and willing to learn from the experience, we may realize that what we are experiencing is actually a gift to prepare us for what God has planned for our future. We must not become bitter at those who wrong us. Without forgiveness, we are imprisoned in hate and unable to learn and grow. If instead of getting angry we look for opportunity, we will be better for it.

Helen Keller was not only deaf, but also blind and mute. To an outside observer, she was completely cut off from the world. At a very early age, due to the extent of her disability, she appeared to be unreachable. If it hadn't been for her parents and her teacher, Anne Sullivan, believing in her and her God-given gifts, then the world would never have been blessed by her.

Helen Keller overcame her challenges to become one of the 20th century's most famous inspirational leaders. She was born on June 27, 1880 in Tuscumbia, Alabama. An illness at age two left her blind, deaf and mute. Her parents hired Anne Sullivan as Helen's Tutor when she was seven, having struggled to communicate with her for years. With Anne's help and patience, she learned how to communicate and eventually even speak.

With Anne's assistance Helen was able to continue her education and attend a school for the deaf. In 1896 she attended the Cambridge school for young ladies, and soon gained notoriety for her ability to overcome the obstacles in her life. She eventually attended Radcliffe college where she graduated Cum Laude. She went on to write books, travel abroad and give many public lectures. She was a strong advocate for the disabled. She was awarded the Medal of Freedom in 1964, and was elected to the women's hall of fame in 1965. She earned honorary doctoral degrees from Temple University and Harvard. Her exemplary life is a powerful testimony of how determination, hard work and imagination can triumph over adversity.

Another person I admire is Napoleon Hill. He has played a big part in helping me to believe that all things are possible. I have been a student of his for many years and have read, listened to, re-read and re-listened to his material until it had become part of my subconscious. He is most known for his best-selling book, *Think and Grow Rich*. I love and often recite one of his famous quotes: "What the mind of man can conceive and believe it can achieve."

I found a way to make that quote my own: "What the mind of Paul can conceive and believe with the unlimited power of God, by faith, Paul can achieve." God has given us many great gifts, one being our minds. Very few of us use that gift wisely. We are often slaves to our emotions and circumstances. In some respect, our minds are the closest link and connection we have with God. Because God is spirit, He doesn't necessarily communicate as we do. My belief is that God not only communicates through His word, the Bible, but through His spirit with our spirit, which in most cases, is our minds. We are called to have the mind of Christ:

"For who has known the mind of the Lord so as to instruct Him? But we have the mind of Christ."
–New International Version, 1 Corinthians 2:16

The mind is a powerful part of who we are, and can be used to bring us both success and absolute destruction. We often become the very things we think about. You can bring in good or bad circumstances—whichever you choose to focus on. If you're driving and you look to the left, you will steer your car to the left. Many people never get the things they want because they focus on the things they don't want, and that is, in fact, what they get.

Certain things happened in Napoleon Hill's life that set the stage for his future decisions. He lost his mother when he was quite young. He misbehaved as a young man, and had a very bad reputation with others. Fortunately, his father remarried, and God saw fit to give Napoleon a loving stepmother who saw good in Napoleon and encouraged him to become better than what others thought of him. She set him on the path to higher achievement and helped him believe in himself.

As a young adult he captured the attention of Andrew Carnegie, who asked Mr. Hill to spend some time with him at his mansion. Mr. Carnegie made Napoleon a proposal and gave him less than two minutes to accept—if he didn't respond, the proposal would be withdrawn. However, Mr. Hill was not made aware of the time limit. Mr. Carnegie tasked him to meet with the most powerful and influential men of his time and interview them about their principles of success. He was told to do this over 20 years, and that, if he accepted, Mr. Carnegie would give him letters of introduction to each of the men. However, Mr. Hill would not be paid a fee for this; only his travel costs would be paid for.

At this point in his life, Mr. Hill did not have much to his name aside from a good work ethic. Mr. Carnegie saw something in Mr. Hill that made him believe that, if he did what he was asked, he would accomplish more and would become more famous than Andrew Carnegie himself. Napoleon Hill accepted and he was blessed, as were the millions of others who have learned from his teachings.

Mr. Hill met with all the great men and women on the list, and documented their keys to success. Millions have benefited from this information, including me. In my study of Napoleon Hill, I came to realize that he was a great man of faith. His son, Blair, was born without ears and thus was deaf from birth. When Mr. Hill was told by doctors about his son's condition, he absolutely dismissed the idea, and stated that his son would someday have 100 percent hearing. Each night for many years Mr. Hill would pray over his son for hours on end, beseeching God to give him his hearing. He would speak the same to his son every day and night. Because of his steadfast faith, his son gained about 40 percent hearing, and years later, with a new hearing aid, had his hearing fully restored. All of this was scientifically impossible, because Blair did not have ears! Blair later turned his disability into a blessing, and went to work for the very company that had restored his hearing.

We can often choose to use our experiences to reveal our purpose in life. Many who have been abused or have struggled with addiction have helped others through the pain they themselves once experienced, and that has become their life mission and purpose.

CHAPTER 6

THE PROCESS OF FINDING OUR PURPOSE— MINING FOR TREASURE TO FIND THE ANSWERS

EVERYTHING THAT HAS BEEN CREATED HAS BEEN CREATED FOR A purpose. Our purpose is discoverable. The difference is that, when *we* create something, we know the intention behind it. Since we did not create ourselves, we may not recognize our purpose right away. I believe our Creator can provide the answers to our searching. We may wish He would make it clear by giving us a set of personalized instructions. In a way, He does. The Bible holds many clues in the scriptures. But the only way to find the purpose that God has hidden within us is to seek Him.

It's like a treasure hunt. He has given us clues, and many of the assessments I provide in this book are your tools for discovering what they are. It's like the California Gold Rush in the mid-1800s. People sold everything to move west in hopes of discovering gold, and many never did. If more people took that same fervency to find the gold within themselves, then more would discover their purpose. Unfortunately, very few do.

Finding your purpose is not easy, and it takes time. Very few people have the necessary discipline to do so. It's easier to settle or remain in ignorance. Putting in the work and discovering your purpose is important for many reasons. Our gifts, talents, passions, personalities and strengths are given to us so we could accomplish very specific things in our lifetime. The reason it is difficult to discover our purpose is a principle in life and nature. The strongest trees are that way because their struggle to endure severe rain and wind has strengthened them. My gymnastics coach used to proudly say, "No pain, no gain." There is truth in that!

In the seeking, and in the struggle, we are developing discipline and discovering ourselves to be found worthy to "wield Excalibur." Our Excalibur is the gift of who we are and why we were created.

Think of the discovery of your purpose as an escape room. The task is to escape by solving multiple puzzles and riddles. The winners are those who figure out the puzzles in the time allotted. I'm not saying that God is a sadistic God who wants to make our search hard. Think about why people do those games. First, the search for clues is challenging and fun. The escape is the reward. In our search for purpose, our escape room is our world. We are not necessarily trying to escape; rather, we are trying to solve the puzzles of who and why we are.

Science fiction fans may remember the movie *The Matrix*. I love that movie for many reasons besides the cool special effects. In that movie, there existed two worlds—the real world where humans were in a battle with the machines, and the fantasy world where the machines created a false world that appeared real. The goal of those who had escaped the fantasy world was to awaken those living in the fantasy world to reality. The fantasy world appeared wonderful, but those who dwelled there were enslaved by their ignorance. Although the real world was harsh and difficult, there was true freedom. I liken that story to what God is trying to do. In *The Matrix*, people viewed Zion as the Promised Land. It is a biblical parallel to the city of Jerusalem. God does not want us to remain ignorant. Two Bible verses best illustrate this:

For what can be known about God is plain to them, because God has shown it to them. For his invisible attributes, namely, his eternal power and divine nature, have been clearly perceived, ever since the creation of the world, in the things that have been made. So they are without excuse.

–English Standard Version, Romans 1:19–20

They are darkened in their understanding and separated from the life of God because of the ignorance that is in them due to the hardening of their hearts. Having lost all sensitivity, they have given themselves over to sensuality to indulge in every kind of impurity, and they are full of greed. That, however, is not the way of life you learned when you heard about Christ and were taught in him in accordance with the truth that is in Jesus.

–New International Version, Ephesians 4:18–21

Morpheus says to Neo, "You take the blue pill, the story ends, you wake up in your bed and believe whatever you want to believe. You take the red pill, you stay in Wonderland, and I show you how deep the rabbit hole goes."

We can choose the "blue pill" and remain in ignorance and struggle through life not knowing why we were created. Or we can choose the "red pill," seek the truth and find our purpose and ultimate fulfillment. The decision is yours.

CHAPTER 7
HOW TO DISCOVER YOUR STRENGTHS

IN THIS CHAPTER, WE ARE GOING TO LOOK AT YOUR STRENGTHS AND how they play into understanding your purpose. As I stated before, no two people are identical. We each possess different strengths and weaknesses.

Unfortunately, many people look to their weaknesses to define themselves. We focus too much on our weaknesses or failures; if we believe them, that will become who we are. Weakness does play a part in who we are overall, but it really shouldn't be a factor in understanding our purpose. Its real function is to help us be aware of our limitations.

When we focus on our strengths, we can use them to fulfill our purpose. Strengths are tasks or actions in which we excel. There are various assessments that can help you identify your strengths. You can also ask others who know you well and have your best interest at heart. It is important to know your strengths so you will be able to use them to serve others. We often do much better with tasks when we are using our strengths. Like in Mother Teresa's case, her strengths were her passion, kindness and compassion, which she used to bless and serve the people of Calcutta.

Many people who use their strengths as intended find they

are much more successful in their careers and relationships. I will be referencing the material and 34 strengths as identified in the Clifton Strengths Assessment. The themes, which sort into four domains, are a culmination of research by Don Clifton, who studied and categorized the talents of the world's most successful people. Together, the themes explain a simple but profound element of human behavior: what's *right* with people. Individually, each theme gives you a way to describe what you naturally do best or what you might need help from others to accomplish.

The four domains are strategic thinking, relationship building, influencing and executing. There are certain strengths that fit into each domain. I will provide a brief description of each. I would encourage you to go to the CliftonStrengths website and take the assessment and identify your strengths (my results were Belief, Intellection, Connectedness, Developer and Includer):

gallup.com/cliftonstrengths

The following descriptions of the Clifton Strengths are found in the book *StrengthsFinder* by Tom Rath:

1. STRATEGIC THINKING

Analytical
They thrive on details and analysis. They want proof! In their desire to get to the truth they may come across as particularly challenging. They are vital in any project as they will root out the problems. They are objective and can appear dispassionate because for them it is about the facts, not the feeling. Their passion is in the details, data and the research.

Context

These are the ones who are more reflective in their thinking and look backward to best understand the present. This allows them to develop the best picture, as they see things from the past for their original intent.

Futuristic

These folks are more future oriented. They can see the finished product by projecting into the future. That future view helps them see what needs to happen in the present to bring that picture about.

Ideation

These folks focus on ideas. They want to know the "why" behind things. They are thrilled when they can come up with an idea that explains things. They think creatively and look at things from a different perspective.

Input

These people are inquisitive. They are collectors, because they are interested in what they collect. They are great learners, especially with things they love.

Intellection

These are the thinkers. They like thinking games, challenging puzzles and problems. They also may be a loner, as they like to ponder and think about things and that's best done alone.

Learner

These folks love to learn new things and grow in their knowledge. They will take classes to further their education.

Strategic

Their goal is to get to the prize or find the best route to the solution. They can see the big picture. This is the coach who stands above the football field to get a better view. They can see alternatives and are able to change the strategy when needed.

2. RELATIONSHIP BUILDING

Adaptability

These people live in the moment. They can adapt as needed to the situation. Flexibility is their middle name.

Connectedness

These people view things from a perspective of interconnectedness. They believe that everything happens for a reason, and there may be a higher purpose. They are very compassionate, caring and accepting. They also may be individuals who rely heavily on faith.

Developer

These are our encouragers. They see the best in people and see their potential. They see the possibilities. They are optimists. The positive ones! They want to see others succeed and that is what charges them. They help others grow and are the cheerleader for others to be their best.

Empathy

They have an uncanny way of reading others emotions and feeling what they are going through. They have the ability to experience life in others' shoes and because of that they are compassionate and caring.

Harmony
These people are the peacemakers. They try to find
commonality to maintain that peace. They do not like
conflict and seek to resolve issues peacefully. They are
respectful of others' views and opinions and seek
harmony in relationships.

Includer
These folks bring others into the group and make them
feel accepted. They are more accepting of others and their
views because they want to feel accepted and included
themselves. They believe that we are all equal.

Individualization
They focus on the uniqueness of others. What makes each
person special, and what makes them "them." They highlight the strengths of others with gifts or comments. They
encourage uniqueness in others.

Positivity
These are the ones to dish out generous praise or
encourage others. They are positive and optimistic. They
see the glass as half full and getting fuller. They are light-
hearted and enjoy fun, and love to laugh.

Relator
They care about creating better relationships. They love
intimacy, feeling close to others and going deep. They're
risk takers when it comes to relationships, knowing their
openness leaves them vulnerable to being hurt.

3. INFLUENCING

Activator
These are the ones on the starting line who jump before

the gun goes off. They are all about action—if we run into problems we will figure it out on the way. They learn as they go.

Command

These are your take-charge leaders. They are very opinionated and have no qualms about expressing their opinion. They're able to move forward with courage no matter how bleak. Their strong leadership may be intimidating to others but most will follow them because of their confidence and courage.

Communication

They have the gift of gab. They can take ideas and concepts and effectively communicate them to others. They love to speak in public to express themselves and are skilled at bringing ideas to life.

Competition

They'll look to others performances to measure their own. They are competitive, trying to beat others in the things they are good at. Their greatest success is when they win. They compare themselves to others, and gain energy in competition. The goal is victory.

Maximizer

They will strive for nothing but excellence—the high achiever who looks to get all "A's," the number one cheerleader or star quarterback. They're always looking to better themselves. These are the ambitious ones.

Self-Assurance

These are the confident ones. They believe in themselves, and have a good understanding of their strengths. These are the fearless ones, who will take risks and face challenges. They tend to be very decisive.

Significance
These are the ones who just want to be accepted and liked. They want to matter to others. It is important that others see them as worthy and important. The desire to be accepted and appreciated is their driving force.

Woo
These are the class clowns or the comedians who are trying to win others over. They do not know a stranger and are very friendly with all. Connection with others is especially important.

4. EXECUTING

Achiever
These are the ones who want medals on their chest or trophies on their shelf. They just want more, and to accomplish more. Their happiness hinges on what they have accomplished or achieved.

Arranger
These are the managers. They can take on complex situations and manage the many variables. They can multi-think and multitask. They like the challenge of figuring out solutions.

Belief

These folks are strong in their beliefs, typically very spiritual, family oriented and ethical. Their beliefs dictate everything about them and the decisions they make. They are very reliable and committed to others. Whatever they do, it must have meaning and connect back to their value system.

Consistency

These people measure their life with a sense of balance and consistency. They try to see everyone as equal, deserving of the same benefits and treatment. Stability is key.

Deliberative

These people need order. They are aware of life's dangers and risks and try to minimize potential problems. They are also very careful in how they approach things and tend to be more reserved.

Discipline

These folks are orderly and like to plan things. Their world needs to be predictable and structured to maintain a sense of control. It must be ordered and planned. They are not big into surprises.

Focus

These people need to know their destination. They are focused on accomplishing what needs to occur to get them there. They are very goal oriented. Their focus helps them to weed out things that will keep them from their goal. Because of their ability to focus, they are very efficient. In a team they are able to keep everyone's eye on the prize.

Responsibility
These people take ownership of their efforts. They are committed and willing to do the hard work to make things happen. They feel bad if they are not able to complete something as it challenges their view of being dependable. These people are doers.

Restorative
These people are problem solvers. They are energized, and kick into high gear when faced with a challenge. They are fixers, and love to bring life into a project and find solutions to problems.

Once you have taken the Clifton Strengths Assessment to identify your strengths, you can use those strengths to be successful not only in your career but in your relationships. It is also very important to learn how to use those strengths to positively influence others. Remember that not everyone has the same strengths. Not all personalities meld well. Success is easier when people are willing to learn more about each other, and take into consideration people's strengths and personalities. This is where awareness of someone's weakness could be balanced by a person's strengths to create harmony.

I have included the strengths as listed in the Clifton Strengths Assessment. You can also find your strengths from other assessments, or by asking those who know you. You can even do a self-assessment. Your strengths are the puzzle pieces of who you are. Your purpose is directly connected to your strengths.

CHAPTER 8
HOW TO DISCOVER YOUR PASSIONS

WHEN I REFER TO PASSIONS, I AM REFERRING TO THINGS YOU LOVE or that excite you. People who are passionate may be very emotional about something they are interested in.

To give you an example, remember Martin Luther King's "I have a dream" speech? Almost everyone who heard it was moved because it exuded passion. He was passionate about the civil rights movement and his actions showed his conviction, even at the cost of imprisonment.

Another example is the passion of Christ. He was passionate in His effort to fulfill his purpose. Indeed, everything He did flowed out of His passion, even offering Himself up to be crucified so that millions could be saved.

Passion is not just an elevated emotional expression; it is so much more. When people are passionate about something, they can spend all day doing something when it seems to have only been seconds. When you are in your passion, there is nothing you would rather do.

Not everyone has tapped into his or her passion. Many have either forgotten or never even bothered to discover it. Children have it naturally, and you see it in their great imaginations during play. Adults have it when they are involved in doing something they absolutely love. Several other examples that come to mind are Thomas Edison, Henry Ford and Steve Jobs. Although very successful, what set them apart was their passion. They loved what they did, and it showed in their creativity and commitment. Some people are passionate about gardening, reading, working out or making money. Knowing your passions is important because it directly relates to knowing your purpose. Passion is like the jet fuel that gets your engine going. Your passions drive you when you want to give up. They remind you why you do what you do.

I love to read. That is one of my passions. I also love to learn and love to teach. My passion for reading allows me to learn, which I can then pass on to others. It fits well in with my other gifts, which you will soon discover. In order to recognize what you are passionate about, write a list of the things you love. Which are most important to you? The goal is to narrow the list down to your top five, then rank them one to five. You may see some patterns emerge. This will help you narrow down truly what is most important to you.

There are five principles to keep in mind as you work to identify your passions:

1. What drives you?
2. What do you care about?
3. What needs will you meet?
4. What cause will you help conquer?
5. What is your ultimate dream?

To help you determine your own passions, take the test at:
thepassiontest.com

CHAPTER 9
HOW TO DISCOVER YOUR LOVE LANGUAGE

WHY IS IT IMPORTANT FOR US TO KNOW AND UNDERSTAND OUR LOVE language, especially as it pertains to our purpose in life? Our love languages represent the way we give and receive love. Finding your purpose has everything to do with service to others, and service to others has everything to do with loving others through action. We must be considerate of the love languages of others. We often try to love others the way we want to be loved, instead of how they want to be loved.

If we know our love language, we know how we best serve and love those we care about. Equally important, we know how we would like others to love and serve us. This helps us understand each other's differences. Understanding these differences can alleviate many potential conflicts.

This assessment will identify how your relational needs are best met. For example, my love language is primarily physical touch. This means I feel love from hugs and soft touch. You can communicate your love language to those close to you, and ask them their own to make sure you are meeting each other's needs. The five love languages identified in Dr. Chapman's book are:

- **Physical Touch:** Someone whose love language is physical touch is best met with touch, hugs and physical presence.
- **Quality Time:** This love language is best expressed by spending time with them and listening. Give them your undivided attention.
- **Words of Affirmation:** These folks' needs are best met through praise, compliments and encouraging words. They like to hear " I love you" or "you're important to me" often.
- **Acts of Service:** These folks love when you do things for them and help them with projects. They appreciate when people serve them out of love.
- **Receiving Gifts:** These people love things that are given to them like flowers, chocolates, letters or cards. They appreciate thoughtfulness, and the time you spent remembering them.

When you discover your love language, be sure to share it with others to help them know how to best serve and love you. Also ensure you find out what their love language is to best love and serve them.

To take Dr. Gary Chapman's love language assessment, visit:
5lovelanguages.com

CHAPTER 10
HOW TO DISCOVER YOUR TEMPERAMENT

Temperament is a person's nature, especially as it affects their permanent behavior. Temperament is formed as a baby, and research has shown that it typically does not change over time. It helps us know how we will react to certain circumstances.

Psychologists have identified four different temperaments: sanguine, phlegmatic, melancholy, and choleric. Hippocrates originally developed the theory of the four temperaments. Most people possess a primary and secondary temperament. The primary temperament is a key component to your personality and how you relate and react to others.

Further information on the study of temperaments can be found in books such as *Spirit Controlled Temperament* by Tim Lahaye; *The Four Tendencies* by Gretchin Rubin; and *Becoming Who We Are* by Mary Rothbart.

To take a temperament test, visit:
psychologia.co

Another test matches the four temperaments to their animal characteristics: Sanguine as the otter, Phlegmatic as the golden retriever, choleric as the lion, and melancholy as the beaver. This information can be found at decal.ga.gov.

THE SANGUINE TEMPERAMENT (OTTER)

Sanguine is the most common temperament, and is just as likely to be found in men as it is in women. Sanguines tend to be talkers, and are more extroverted. They come across as carefree, easy going and social. They may also come across as the strong leader type who will take charge of a situation or conversation. They are very people-oriented. They typically exhibit a wide range of emotions and behaviors. They can be playful and impulsive. They are fun to be around as they have a good sense of humor and keep things lively. They are expressive and affectionate towards others. They are good at building relationships and are typically trusting of others. They are extremely competitive and can come across as aggressive when in competition. They thrive on attention, and are fearful of making a bad impression or being rejected.

Sanguine are often sociable, outgoing, optimistic, forgiving, confident, fun loving and goal oriented. Sanguine can also be impulsive, often late, selfish, forgetful and have a tendency to exaggerate. Typical jobs for otters are sales, customer service, marketing, public relations, travel and entertainment.

The sanguine personality is highly affected by a chemical called dopamine, which makes these people intensely curious and creative. Their curiosity can be expressed in their love for reading and pursuing different kinds of knowledge. Sanguine people usually possess high amounts of energy, so they may seem restless and spontaneous.

This type of personality loves the life of luxury; they like to impress others with their expensive clothes, designer accessories and flashy cars. If choleric people thrive on the money-making process itself, sanguine people know how to enjoy money, luxury and comfort like nobody else. They are big spenders. If they can afford it, they travel a lot. They are likely to stay in splendid hotels, enjoying exciting safaris and luxury cruises, deriving full happiness and pleasure from their wealth. They will indulge in their rich, comfortable and sumptuous living effectively ignoring the world's problems and crises.

People with a sanguine personality are willing to take risks for the sake of pursuit of their diverse interests. These people feel bored if they are not absorbed by something intriguing. Their constant cravings for adventure and novelty are the primary motivating force behind their actions.

People with a sanguine personality adapt quickly and can play many roles. Buoyant, lively and optimistic, they can absolutely charm the pants off anyone that seeks their attention. Their need for variety and luxury explains why they prefer to live in big cities. Sanguine people cannot tolerate boredom. Routine jobs, repetitive experiences and dull companions annoy them. For the most part, they will try to avoid routine and monotony at all costs. Even more so, they thrive on interruptions because they are energized by changes in course.

These people are impulsive, and they will often find it difficult to control their cravings. They may struggle with weight. More than any other types of personality, this temperament is more susceptible to smoking, alcohol, drugs, gambling and risky behaviors. Their spontaneity reflects in last-minute plans and moments of intellectual discovery. Sanguine people are usually more creative than other types, be it poetry, music, theater, art, business or cooking. Sadly, they are also most susceptible to chemical imbalances, addictions and mood disorders.

People of this type seem to be hungry for knowledge—some of them are walking encyclopedias, while some others visit almost every country in the world. Many stay in school years and years after their peers have graduated. They will do almost anything to satisfy their always present need to be absorbed by something meaningful and exciting. As a result, they will often end up having several degrees. However, sanguine people are so busy with their many interests that they are prone to procrastination. They are too busy to think about deadlines and finishing one task before going ahead to begin another.

These people are very autonomous and unconventional. They trust their impulses and take risks. Their motto is: "Nothing ventured, nothing gained." They launch into projects that seem sure to fail but somehow always manage to win big. People with a sanguine personality are extreme optimists who make it their job to seek joy. They are sensation seekers that derive pleasure from highly arousing experiences; they enjoy life to the fullest.

THE PHLEGMATIC TEMPERAMENT (GOLDEN RETRIEVER)

Phlegmatic temperaments are also common. The phlegmatic is almost the opposite of sanguine temperaments. Many people may have a primary of sanguine and secondary of phlegmatic, or vice versa. The primary is the most dominant of the two. Individuals who are more on the phlegmatic side are those that like to serve others. They are very giving and sensitive to the needs of others. They are charitable with their time and resources.

They are more introverted in their approach. They typically do not have a lot of friends, but those friends they do have are incredibly special to them; they are loyalists. They are typically not aggressive, and would be considered the peacemakers. They do not want to make waves. They are easy to get along with as they are very caring of others. They are not the best at making decisions as they do not want to stand out or appear to be disagreeable. They also thrive on stability, routine and do not respond well to change. They are very warm, and life typically centers around home and family.

The strengths of the phlegmatic are they are calm, reliable, diplomatic, content, accepting, rational, loyal, loving and peacemakers. The weaknesses of the phlegmatic are they are shy, passive, indecisive, permissive, unambitious, apathetic and avoid conflict. Typical jobs for the phlegmatic are nursing, education, human and social services and counseling.

People with phlegmatic personalities are unassuming, agreeable and intuitive. They possess the ability of "web thinking;" the ability to see the relationship between many bits of data they collect. They have an incredible skill to gather facts, classify them into different categories and then see the relationship between seemingly contradictory elements. Essentially, they are able to read between the lines. Phlegmatic men and women do not do very well at memorizing separate unrelated facts. They grow bored and annoyed. To be excited by the process, they need to be able to generalize.

It's all about the estrogen! Phlegmatic personality traits are linked to estrogen, which is present in both men and women. However, phlegmatic people are predominantly females. Millions of nerve fibers connect the two hemispheres of the brain, and estrogen builds more nerve connections between the remote areas within each region. These connections help with big picture thinking. These people are imaginative; they like to think abstractly.

They will try to read your body language and tell you what you are thinking. Phlegmatic want to know other people's deepest feelings, and strive to build intimate attachments with everyone in their lives. They are interested in cooperation and interpersonal harmony, and therefore they preserve their family ties and friendships. When there is a conflict, they seek to satisfy the needs of everyone involved. These men and women are very empathetic and compassionate.

People with a phlegmatic personality are very agreeable. Phlegmatic could be described as cooperative, considerate, charitable, sympathetic, trusting and warm. They like to express their feelings, sometimes dramatizing their experience, which is evidence of high estrogen activity. Phlegmatic men and women seek to contribute to society at large. They strive to fight cancer, donate to orphanages and help the poor. They also strive for greater self-knowledge, which they see as a must.

On the negative side, people with a phlegmatic personality can be indecisive and unable to focus on essential details. They keep ruminating on the bigger picture while ignoring the crucial aspects. Their talkativeness can be annoying, and because they seek connection, they may appear needy or in constant demand of reassurance. They may be trying to understand you, but they also may assume that you see and feel the world the same way they do. They might take criticisms as an insult and pout for days, weeks or months. They are very prone to depression.

THE MELANCHOLY TEMPERAMENT (BEAVER)

The melancholy are incredibly detailed oriented and organized. They have a strong need to do things by the book. They are the ones who will read and follow the instructions. They are also "doers," and get things done. They are who you want doing quality control. They are very task oriented and have a strong need to be right and get things done correctly. They are typically good listeners and communicate details.

They are not the best at making decisions unless they have everything they need to make the right choice, as they are fearful of being wrong. They also avoid pressure and tense situations, because being rushed increases the likelihood of mistakes. They work best with clearly defined tasks with plenty of time to plan, strategize and implement. They tend to be perfectionists, and when pressured or in an unfamiliar situation they can become aggressive in their response. They are private and introverted in their approach to others.

Melancholies are logical, factual and analytical. They also tend to be worriers because they want to do everything right. They have high expectations because of their perfectionistic nature and thus can be demanding of others. They are also very conscientious and suspicious of others. They are not the most trusting of others until they feel the person can be trusted, so it is hard for them to form relationships. The strengths of the melancholy are they are accurate, analytical, detail-oriented, thorough, industrious, orderly, methodical, intuitive and controlled. The weaknesses are they are too hard on themselves, critical of others, perfectionistic, overly cautious, will not make decisions without all the facts, picky and overly sensitive.

Typical career choices for the melancholy may be research, art, science, accounting, administration and social work. Men and women with melancholic personality share many traits— they tend to be loyal to their family and friends and extremely careful. Respectability and moral issues are particularly important to them; they prefer to follow societal norms and family traditions. They are respectful to authority, follow the rules and feel comfortable in hierarchies where structure, regulations and order are implemented.

They want to be a part of the larger community. They see their loyalty as a duty. Melancholic personality traits are associated with serotonin, which suppresses aggressive tendencies. That explains why melancholic people are calm, self-confident, deeply attached to their family and community and loyal. They are very orderly and do not like unpredictability—they enjoy making definite plans and keeping schedules. They love routine, which they find relaxing. Repetitive motion increases serotonin levels. It is relaxing in its nature, but nobody enjoys it more than a melancholic!

These people pay attention to detail; they remember special dates, anniversaries and events. They will remember details about their neighbors and colleagues. Melancholics do not see family and social ties as something that limits their freedom and flexibility as can happen with sanguines or cholerics. To them, these are safety nets—a soft place to fall but on a much grander scale. It adds meaning to their life. Since society and family ties are such an essential part of their daily lifestyles and routines, they absolutely cannot see themselves without it. Take this away from them, and they will be devastated. That is why the melancholic is not likely to be somebody who would marry a foreigner or leave to another country for permanent residence.

Melancholics need to be orderly, even in their speech. They will express themselves precisely and accurately, providing all the relevant information. If you interrupt them or ask them a question, they will think you are not interested in what they are talking about. Unlike sanguines, they hate distractions and get frustrated by them. If you want to impress them, do not talk about your big ideas. Instead, give them precise information and stick to the details.

Their need for order is expressed even in their jokes; they will not be a fan of nonsense humor. Even their jokes reflect order, predictability and closure. People with a melancholic personality are thorough and accurate. They are process-oriented and like to pursue their goals in a precise, straightforward way. Before they start a specific task, they need to organize themselves and break down the task into manageable steps. An average melancholic is not the kind of person that will work well under pressure.

Melancholics are persistent and patient. They do not get bored easily and excel at tasks that require attention and repetition. Their orderliness is also reflected in their tastes. Melancholics love geometric designs that are simple, orderly, predictable, repetitive and symmetrical. If you give a melancholic man one striped shirt and one hundred shirts with an asymmetrical design, he will be wearing that one striped shirt every day. Asymmetry makes them uncomfortable. However, most people are a mix of several personality types that make them much more flexible.

These people make excellent managers and administrators because they follow the rules and stick to the facts. Even more so, they are reliable, and make it a point to maintain social ties. They are superb at managing people, whether it is at work or at home. One of their strongest needs is the need to belong, and this is why they want to be reliable, respectable and charitable. Their emotional well-being depends on their social networks.

Melancholics are proud of their accomplishments—they will display their trophies, medals, diplomas, certificates and photos with influential people. Generally, they want to do things in an accepted way; they prefer to plan things in advance and to know ahead of time what they are going to do. On the negative side, people with a melancholic personality may become close-minded, dogmatic and stubborn. They also tend to turn to pessimism which may turn into fatalism, believing that nothing will ever change for better. Sometimes they get overly critical and judgmental because they often believe in their own moral superiority. Their frugality may turn into stinginess. Some melancholics can become fixated on the past. They can ruminate for hours how their life would be if they made different choices. Hoarding is quite a common problem.

THE CHOLERIC TEMPERAMENT (LION)

Those with the temperament of choleric are very results-oriented. They make goals and they stick to them. They are driven to succeed and can be aggressive in their attempts. They face opposition head-on with the mindset of getting results. They are confident and self-reliant. They are extroverted by nature. They are strong leaders and others look to them for guid-ance. They are strong-willed and independent. They are assertive, and communicate directly. They are risk takers and get bored easily. They are usually the leaders or bosses at work. They are problem solvers and look for challenging opportunities. They will take charge in situations if no one else does.

Most choleric are entrepreneurs. They are also your visionar-ies. In relationships, they can be dominant and sometimes domi-neering. They make decisions quickly, which can be problematic at times. They find it easy to make decisions, not only for them-selves but for others. They are highly creative, but do not always think through the details. Choleric are very compassionate people in social settings but have some difficulties in personal relationships, due to challenges empathizing with others. The choleric strengths are they are decisive, goal-oriented, achievement-driven, independent, self-starters, persistent, efficient and competitive. The weaknesses are they are impatient, blunt, poor listeners, impulsive, demanding, insensitive to the feelings of others, quickly bored by routine and view projects as more important than people.

Typical jobs for choleric are business, law, technology, security, management and engineering. The choleric personality type is associated with testosterone, and although every temperament is represented by members of both genders, most choleric people are men. Generally, cholerics are money and success-oriented. They are fascinated by stocks, investments, money markets and all kinds of revenue generation methods, the way others are fascinated by art and poetry. These people are very practical, and they make for naturally gifted businesspeople. Continually looking for opportunities and always working on themselves, they build successful businesses that thrive and benefit others. That does not mean that these people are greedy for money by any means! From their perspective, work is fun. However, they never do well in a subordinate position; they are all about independence, financially and otherwise.

Another unique quality of choleric people is their ability to systematize everything. That is why they usually enjoy math and other exact sciences. They have a hard time trying to understand why the approach they use when solving a math problem cannot be used when addressing relationship issues.

Testosterone also contributes to their spatial skills. Their spatial skills can be reflected in musical and athletic ability, particularly sports that require spatial skills, such as soccer. They are goal-oriented and have a sharp focus as they work. Their concentration is deep and narrow. When they are busy with something, cholerics are simply not capable of noticing other things that are going on around them. This type of person is very analytical and logical. These people are kings and queens of figuring things out.

High testosterone activity in these men and women makes them very straightforward. Generally, choleric people do not strive to be polite, respectful or friendly. They do stuff according to what is convenient to them and, most importantly, in line with their goals. Wasting words and repeating the obvious is pointless to them. Forcing them to do so is a surefire way to annoy them! Choleric personality is characterized by pragmatism, and it is typical for them to make their decisions fast and act immediately. Unlike many others, they don't have a problem when offered multiple choices. They prefer to prove themselves with action and put the talk aside. You will hardly hear a choleric going on and on about what he is planning to do, like as often happens with sanguine-phlegmatic. This kind of behavior is annoying to cholerics.

Although you might think cholerics are boring and have nothing to share, the fact of the matter is that they often are the ones who have the most fun (alone). Years pass, and you could be amazed at what they have achieved. It is no wonder why they are how they are. Choleric people have everything they need to excel in business, sports and science. They are naturally predisposed to set goals then reach them, believing in reasoning, logic and investigation.

They are skeptical and do not trust easily. Cholerics need to investigate the facts on their own, then analyze them. People with a choleric personality have excellent problem-solving skills and as long as they are satisfied with the reasoning behind their strategy, they act bold and are self-confident. Both confidence and daring arise from high testosterone. They have no problem tolerating long hours of work and isolation to reach a goal.

Highly independent people without much respect for diplomas and other credentials, they are armed with their autonomy and independence. Both choleric men and women are likely to be highly competitive, almost to the point of being aggressive, which is another sign of high testosterone activity. People with this temperament are determined to succeed. However, they are rarely satisfied with the time and effort they spend on their projects. They keep on raising the bar to the point where many of them live with the constant worry that one day, they will fail. Once they disappoint themselves, they will blame themselves ruthlessly. However, choleric people never give up their attempts to succeed.

They love knowledge and look for intelligent partners. Otherwise, they generally avoid socializing unless they are interested in the conversation, which of course should be somehow related to their goals. This temperamental makeup is typically characterized by detachment from their feelings because they admire emotional control. Choleric strive to be logical, analytical, competent, just and convincing. They usually appear calm and collected. They do not smile much and avoid eye contact, and despite their best efforts at total self-control, they might "lose it" sometimes and explode into rage.

COMPATIBILITY OF TEMPERAMENTS

Phlegmatics and melancholics are very compatible; their temperaments balance each other. Melancholies are also compatible with other melancholies. Sanguines and melancholies are direct opposites that would require a lot of effort, but have the potential to be a good match. Cholerics and melancholics would not be a good match due to conflicts between traits. Sanguines and phlegmatics can be a good match due to the phlegmatic's wariness of the sanguine's impetuous passion. Two cholerics understand each other with no words.

The sanguine and choleric match is rare. They are attracted to attributes of each other's personality but often suppress each other's freedom. Phlegmatics and cholerics are a good match as they balance each other well. Two phlegmatics together can create a love story like none other.

All temperaments have the potential to succeed together if they each learn to appreciate their differences and encourage one another. The different types do not always mesh well. It is possible that two people of quite different temperaments may have difficulties in relationships. While temperament cannot be changed, you can learn to understand each other and learn ways to cope with each others' needs.

The way you perceive the world around you has a direct impact on how you interact with it. Armed with more knowledge about your temperament, you can cultivate more awareness around your personality and what it means for you in your daily life. Awareness is always the first step in cultivating change. If you have a temperament that tends to lean more towards the negative or prevents you from taking chances, you might want to develop a more positive outlook on life. Being more positive will give you the ability to thrive without fear holding you back from fully experiencing or enjoying the world. Just make sure you are always realistic in your positivity, or you run the risk of disappointing yourself and hindering your progress.

CHAPTER 11

HOW TO DISCOVER YOUR PERSONALITY STYLE

THE PERSONALITY STYLE-PERSONALITY DISORDER CONTINUUM

Style		Disorder
Conscientious	⟷	Obsessive-Compulsive
Self-Confident	⟷	Narcissistic
Dramatic	⟷	Histrionic
Vigilant	⟷	Paranoid
Mercurial	⟷	Borderline
Devoted	⟷	Dependent
Solitary	⟷	Schizoid
Leisurely	⟷	Passive-Aggressive
Sensitive	⟷	Avoidant
Idiosyncratic	⟷	Schizotypal
Adventurous	⟷	Antisocial
Self-Sacrificing	⟷	Self-Defeating
Aggressive	⟷	Sadistic
Serious	⟷	Depressive

Your personality is a distinctive pattern of how you think, feel and behave that makes you who you are. The New Personality Self-Portrait 25 (found at *npsp25.com*) delineates 14 personality styles which, in each person's unique combination, shape the way you lead a productive and satisfying life, adapt to change and problem-solve. The test will show what personality style you lean towards. This is extremely helpful in understanding how you think, feel and behave.

The traits exhibited on the left side of the table reflect a healthy state of mind, where we are functioning well and in a state of balance. We exhibit the traits on the right when we are in states of stress and worry. I recommend we monitor our moods and identify the triggers that lead us towards the column on the right. Deep breathing, relaxation and meditation can help. Diet and exercise are also positive ways to manage your state.

Your results will describe your personality style. The descriptions of each personality style below can also be found in the book *New Personality Self-Portrait* by John M. Oldman.

Conscientious: Hard-working, detail-oriented, persevering, invested in rightness, perfectionist, prudent, order-loving and intellectual.

Self-Confident: Self-assured, entitled, ambitious, political, competitive, successful, poised and charming.

Dramatic: Emotional, colorful, attentive, attractive, seductive, trusting, intuitive, spontaneous and imaginative.

Vigilant: Independent, cautious, perceptive, defensive, reactive to criticism and loyal.

Mercurial: Intense, passionate, reactive, romantic, impulsive, creative, imaginative, demanding, needy and changeable.

Devoted: Deeply attached and committed, deferential, considerate, cooperative, polite and preferring membership to leadership.

Solitary: Comfortable alone, independent, unsentimental, stoic and self-contained.

Leisurely: Independent, easygoing, pleasure-seeking, resistant to demands, self-accepting, stubborn and family-oriented.

Sensitive: Reserved, discreet, concerned about expectations, comfortable with routine and familiarity, self-controlled and spontaneous when secure.

Idiosyncratic: Unconventional, spiritual, speculative, inner-directed and original.

Adventurous: Nonconforming, risk-loving, self-reliant, persuasive, courageous, spontaneous, on-the-move and unworried.

Self-Sacrificing: Generous, deferential, altruistic, nonjudgmental, humble, long-suffering and naive.

Aggressive: Comfortable with power, hierarchical, responsible, disciplined, goal-directed, brave, physically active and assertive.

Serious: Sober, unpretentious, accountable, responsible, ruminative, prepared for all consequences, dependable and contrite.

PAUL P'S SELF PORTRAIT

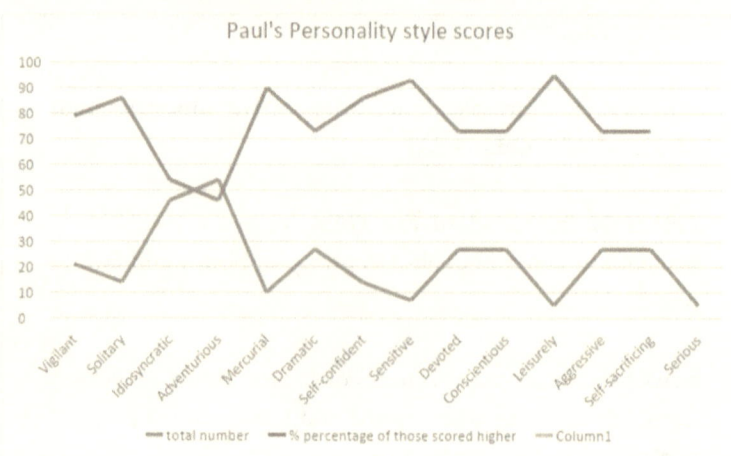

Paul's Personality style scores

The graph above shows my raw scores and how they compared to the rest of the people who took this test. The higher the red bar, the lower my score is relative to the rest of the world. As my results show, I'm more idiosyncratic and adventurous but less mercurial, sensitive, leisurely and serious.

Once you understand your top personality styles, you can focus on how to highlight them to enhance your personality and embrace who *you* are. It's also important to be mindful of triggers that may take you towards the negative side of that personality style. These personality styles have a yin–yang factor and you need to know the positive and negative nature of both to minimize the negative and enhance the positive.

CHAPTER 12
HOW TO DISCOVER
YOUR PERSONALITY TYPE

I HAVE FOUND THE RESEARCH DONE BY MYERS-BRIGGS TO BE extremely helpful, and have included the website and personality assessment in this chapter. This test will determine which of the 16 personality types best applies to you.

Your personality type plays a large role in your personal and professional relationships. For example, someone who is an introvert may not be the best in sales, and a thinker may not be the best as a counselor. There are four main categories in the Myers-Briggs personality assessment:

1. I (INTROVERTS) VERSUS E (EXTROVERTS)

- Introverts typically like to work and be alone, and like to focus on one thing at a time.
- Extroverts are energized by being with people, are multitaskers and prefer working at a quick pace.

2. T (THINKERS) VERSUS F (FEELERS)

- Thinkers tend to make decisions using analysis and research.
- Feelers are more sensitive and base many of their decisions on the emotions of themselves and others.

3. S (SENSORS) VERSUS N (INTUITIVES)

- Sensors focus on facts, details and common sense to come up with solutions to problems.
- Intuitives focus on big pictures and seek creative solutions.

4. J (JUDGES) VERSUS P (PERCEIVERS)

- Judges are highly organized and prepared. They like to stick to plans and follow rules.
- Perceivers are more spontaneous and flexible with their plans.

After taking the assessment, you will end up with a pattern of four letters (I/E, T/F, S/N, J/P). This pattern will give further insight into how you think, relate, process and decide things.

What's Your Personality Type?

ISTJ	ISFJ	INFJ	INTJ
Responsible, sincere, analytical, reserved, realistic, systematic. Hardworking and trustworthy with sound practical judgement.	Warm, considerate, gentle, responsible, pragmatic, thorough. Devoted caretakers who enjoy being helpful to others.	Idealistic, organized, insightful, dependable, compassionate, gentle. Seek harmony and cooperation, enjoy intellectual stimulation.	Innovative, independent, strategic, logical, reserved, insightful. Driven by their own original ideas to achieve improvements.
ISTP	**ISFP**	**INFP**	**INTP**
Action-oriented, logical, analytical, spontaneous, reserved, independent. Enjoy adventure, skilled at understanding how mechanical things work.	Gentle, sensitive, nurturing, helpful, flexible, realistic. Seek to create a personal environment that is both beautiful and practical.	Sensitive, creative, idealistic, perceptive, caring, loyal. Value inner harmony and personal growth, focus on dreams and possibilities.	Intellectual, logical, precise, reserved, flexible, imaginative. Original thinkers who enjoy speculation and creative problem solving.
ESTP	**ESFP**	**ENFP**	**ENTP**
Outgoing, realistic, action-oriented, curious, versatile, spontaneous. Pragmatic problem solvers and skillful negotiators.	Playful, enthusiastic, friendly, spontaneous, tactful, flexible. Have strong common sense, enjoy helping people in tangible ways.	Enthusiastic, creative, spontaneous, optimistic, supportive, playful. Value inspiration, enjoy starting new projects, see potential in others.	Inventive, enthusiastic, strategic, enterprising, inquisitive, versatile. Enjoy new ideas and challenges, value inspiration.
ESTJ	**ESFJ**	**ENFJ**	**ENTJ**
Efficient, outgoing, analytical, systematic, dependable, realistic. Like to run the show and get things done in an orderly fashion.	Friendly, outgoing, reliable, conscientious, organized, practical. Seek to be helpful and please others, enjoy being active and productive..	Caring, enthusiastic, idealistic, organized. Skilled communicators who value connection with people.	Strategic, logical, efficient, outgoing, ambitious, independent. Effective organizers of people and long-range planners.

WHAT'S YOUR MYERS-BRIGGS TYPE?

Use the questions on the next page to determine the four letters of your Myers-Briggs type. For each pair of letters, choose the side that seems most natural to you, even if you don't agree with every description.

1. Are you outwardly or inwardly focused? If you:

• Could be described as talkative, outgoing • Like to be in a fast-paced environment • Tend to work out ideas with others, think out loud • Enjoy being the center of attention	• Could be described as reserved, private • Prefer a slower pace with time for contemplation • Tend to think things through inside your head • Would rather observe than be the center of attention
then you prefer **E**-xtraversion	*then you prefer* **I**-ntroversion

2. How do you prefer to take in information? If you:

• Focus on the reality of how things are • Pay attention to concrete facts and details • Prefer ideas that have practical applications • Like to describe things in a specific, literal way	• Imagine the possibilities of how things could be • Notice the big picture, see how everything connects • Enjoy ideas and concepts for their own sake • Like to describe things in a figurative, poetic way
then you prefer **S**-ensing	*then you prefer* i-**N**-tuition

3. How do you prefer to make decisions? If you:

• Make decisions in an impersonal way, using logical reasoning • Value justice, fairness • Enjoy finding the flaws in an argument • Could be described as reasonable, level-headed	• Base your decisions on personal values and how your actions affect others • Value harmony, forgiveness • Like to please others and point out the best in people • Could be described as warm, empathetic
then you prefer **T**-hinking	*then you prefer* **F**-eeling

4. How do you prefer to live your outer life? If you:

• Prefer to have matters settled • Think rules and deadlines should be respected • Prefer to have detailed, step-by-step instructions • Make plans, want to know what you're getting into	• Prefer to leave your options open • See rules and deadlines as flexible • Like to improvise and make things up as you go • Are spontaneous, enjoy surprises and new situations
then you prefer **J**-udging	*then you prefer* **P**-erceiving

CHAPTER 13
HOW TO DISCOVER YOUR GIFTS AND TALENTS

OUR GIFTS AND TALENTS MAKE US WHO WE ARE. THEY GIVE US AN insight into our uniqueness. They help us understand what we are supposed to do, and who we are supposed to be. How many of us have heard about someone who was naturally gifted or naturally talented? Some people are naturals, and others have to train. It may not come naturally for everyone. Some people have God-given gifts. Michael Jordan was naturally gifted, but he practiced relentlessly to perfect his gift and become one of the best basketball players of all time. Gifts and talents often flow from our passion. If we have passion, we often do it over and over until we master it. In our pursuit of passion we often discover our gifts and talents.

My son Lane is naturally gifted with music and photography. He just has a knack for it. Often we have to try a lot of things before we find our talents. When you find it, your passion will drive you to mastery, mentorship and service. Don't allow others' opinions to sway you from your path. Do what you love and love what you do.

Knowing our gifts and talents is the key to understanding our purpose. Talents typically are related to techniques or skills. For example, we may be talented in music, art or engineering.

Gifts are typically related to the spirit or soul, as related to service. Gifts energize us; they are our natural bent.

John Holland, who developed the Holland Code Assessment, theorizes that people's interests can be categorized into six areas of preference:

Realistic (R): These people like to fix things. They are practical, reliable and modest. They like to take risks and are outdoorsy, athletic and mechanical.

Investigative (I): These people are independent, self-motivated, creative, original, intellectual, curious, introspective, inventors and researchers.

Artistic (A): These people are flexible, nonconformist, original, imaginative, free spirited, creative and artistic or musically talented.

Social (S): These people are friendly, cheerful, and kind. They like to teach. They are generous, good listeners, cooperative, social and interested in others.

Enterprising (E): These people are natural-born leaders and risk takers. They are optimistic, self-confident, ambitious, persuasive and influential.

Conventional (C): These people are practical, methodical, efficient, responsible, conscientious, organized and careful. They like routine and detail.

CHAPTER 14

HOW TO DISCOVER
YOUR SPIRITUAL GIFT

SPIRITUAL GIFTS ARE GIFTS GIVEN TO US BY GOD TO ENHANCE OUR natural abilities and allow us to more effectively serve others. We exist in a triune state: body, soul and spirit. Genesis illustrates this for us:

> *"Then the Lord God formed a man from the dust of the ground and breathed into his nostrils the breath of life, and man became a living soul."*
> —New International Version, Genesis 2:7

This means we have gifts of the body, gifts of the soul and gifts of the spirit. An artist, sculptor or athlete possesses gifts of the body. A singer, songwriter, poet, counselor or orator possesses gifts of the soul. A teacher, leader, preacher or healer possesses gifts of the spirit. Some spiritual gifts could be considered supernatural, such as healings, miracles or prophecy.

God will give you tests to help you determine your gifts so that you may better help others with them. Christ says:

"You shall love the Lord your God with all your heart, and with all your soul, and with all your strength and with all your mind, and your neighbor as yourself."
  –English Standard Version, Luke 10:27

From a Christian perspective, the human spirit is the very core of the person's being and the essential seat of his or her existence. There is a common belief that when the body dies, the spirit lives on as a nonphysical entity.

The body, or flesh, is our physical reality—our arms, legs and internal organs. The soul is a little more complicated, because it comprises the mental and emotional aspects of being human: reason, character, feelings, consciousness, memory, perception and thinking. These are intangible parts. This is where our personality and temperament originates. The soul, through the working mechanism of the body, enables us to live. When the body dies, the soul lives on, because it is not dependent on the physical or natural elements that sustain the body.

When humans rebelled and disobeyed God, the soul continued to exist, but it is believed that the spirit in humans died, separating us from God and preventing us from having the relationship for which we were created. For example, Jesus says in John 3:1-2 that we must be born again (of the spirit), indicating its previous death. The reason God offered up His son on the cross as a sacrifice was to restore that relationship with God. When a person accepts the sacrifice that God offered in Christ Jesus, and believes in Him, that person will be saved (or born again in the spirit). They will put their faith in Christ and follow Him and His ways, which are outlined in the New Testament. The Bible states that when a person believes, the Holy Spirit— God in Spirit form, and the third element of the Trinity—enters them to guide their life in obedience to God's commandments. The Holy Spirit gives each believer a spiritual gift that can be used to do the work that God has planned for them. That gift is the tool that God uses to bless others.

Finally, spiritual gifts are abilities given by the Holy Spirit to each believer to create community, growing into the fullness of the character of Jesus Christ.

POTENTIAL SPIRITUAL GIFTS ACCORDING TO KEY BIBLE PASSAGES

1. New International Version, Romans 12: 4-8:

For just as each of us has one body with many members, and these members do not all have the same function, so in Christ we, though many, form one body, and each member belongs to all the others. We have different gifts, according to the grace given to each of us. If your gift is prophesying, then prophesy in accordance with your faith; if it is serving, then serve; if it is teaching, then teach; if it is to encourage, then give encouragement; if it is giving, then give generously; if it is to lead, do it diligently; if it is to show mercy, do it cheerfully.

Spiritual Gifts: Exhortation, Giving, Leadership, Mercy, Prophecy, Service and Teaching.

2. New International Version, 1 Corinthians 12:

Now about the gifts of the Spirit, brothers and sisters, I do not want you to be uninformed. You know that when you were pagans, somehow or other you were influenced and led astray to mute idols. Therefore I want you to know that no one who is speaking by the Spirit of God says, "Jesus be cursed," and no one can say, "Jesus is Lord," except by the Holy Spirit.

There are different kinds of gifts, but the same Spirit distributes them. There are different kinds of service, but the same Lord. There are different kinds of working, but in all of them and in everyone it is the same God at work.

Now to each one the manifestation of the Spirit is given for the common good. To one there is given through the Spirit a message of wisdom, to another a message of knowledge by means of the same Spirit, to another faith by the same Spirit, to another gifts of healing by that one Spirit, to another miraculous powers, to another prophecy, to another distinguishing between spirits, to another speaking in different kinds of tongues, and to still another the interpretation of tongues. All these are the work of one and the same Spirit, and he distributes them to each one, just as he determines.

Just as a body, though one, has many parts, but all its many parts form one body, so it is with Christ. For we were all baptized by one Spirit so as to form one body—whether Jews or Gentiles, slave or free—and we were all given the one Spirit to drink. Even so the body is not made up of one part but of many.

Now if the foot should say, "Because I am not a hand, I do not belong to the body," it would not for that reason stop being part of the body. And if the ear should say, "Because I am not an eye, I do not belong to the body," it would not for that reason stop being part of the body. If the whole body were an eye, where would the sense of hearing be? If the whole body were an ear, where would the sense of smell be? But in fact God has placed the parts in the body, every one of them, just as he wanted them to be. If they were all one part, where would the body be? As it is, there are many parts, but one body.

The eye cannot say to the hand, "I don't need you!" And the head cannot say to the feet, "I don't need you!" On the contrary, those parts of the body that seem to be weaker are indispensable, and the parts that we think are less honorable we treat with special honor. And the parts that are unpresentable are treated with special modesty, while our presentable parts need no special treatment. But God has put the body together, giving greater honor to the parts that lacked it, so that there should be no division in the body, but that its parts should have equal concern for each other. If one part suffers, every part suffers with it; if one part is honored, every part rejoices with it.

Now you are the body of Christ, and each one of you is a part of it. And God has placed in the church first of all apostles, second prophets, third teachers, then miracles, then gifts of healing, of helping, of guidance, and of different kinds of tongues. Are all apostles? Are all prophets? Are all teachers? Do all work miracles? Do all have gifts of healing? Do all speak in tongues? Do all interpret? Now eagerly desire the greater gifts.

Spiritual Gifts: Administration, Apostle, Discernment, Faith, Healings, Helps, Knowledge, Miracles, Prophecy, Teaching, Tongues, Tongues Interpretation and Wisdom.

3. New International Version, Ephesians 4:

So Christ himself gave the apostles, the prophets, the evangelists, the pastors and teachers, to equip his people for works of service, so that the body of Christ may be built up until we all reach unity in the faith and in the knowledge of the Son of God and become mature, attaining to the whole measure of the fullness of Christ.

Spiritual Gifts: Apostle, Evangelism, Pastor, Prophecy and Teaching.

DEFINITIONS OF SPIRITUAL GIFTS AND THEIR CORRESPONDING SCRIPTURES

To get a better understanding of each spiritual gift, each one is explained below with an accompanying passage from Scripture. Also important is that some spiritual gifts are closely related to one another, specifically the spiritual gifts of Power (Faith, Healings, Miracles), Ministry (Apostle, Evangelism, Prophecy), Manifestation (Prophecy, Tongues, Interpretation of Tongues) and Revelation (Discernment, Knowledge, Wisdom). These related gifts are also marked in the list below:

Administration: 1 Corinthians 12:28—Directs others towards God's will through planning, organizing and supervising. They have strong organizational abilities.

Apostle (Ministry): Ephesians 4:11; 1 Corinthians 12:28—Called to spread God's word to others, are good leaders and are sensitive to spiritual matters.

Discernment (Revelation): 1 Corinthians 12:10—Can see the difference between truth and error and can differentiate between good and evil in others.

Evangelism (Ministry): Ephesians 4:11—Called to speak about God to others.

Exhortation: Romans 12:8—Provide comfort, counsel and encouragement to others.

Faith (Power): 1 Corinthians 12:8–10—Walk not by sight but by a complete trust in God, boldly holding firm to God's promises.

Giving: Romans 12:8—Generous and freely give where there is need.

Healings (Power): 1 Corinthians 12:9, 28, 30—Supernatural power to heal through faith, and help others believe in God's ability to heal.

Helps: 1 Corinthians. 12:28—Seek to serve others and assist where there is need.

Hospitality: 1 Peter 4:9, 10—Warmly welcoming people, even strangers, into one's home or church as a means of serving those in need of food or lodging.

Knowledge (Revelation): 1 Corinthians 12:8—Students of the Bible seeking to fully understand His word.

Leadership: Romans 12:8—Leaders or shepherds with the responsibility to lead other believers.

Mercy: Romans 12:8—Caring, empathetic, and compassionate of others' needs. They can relate emotionally to others and feel another's pain and provide comfort.

Miracles (Power): 1 Corinthians 12:10, 28—Similar to those with the gift of healing, they can tap into things that are typically not possible through the power of God. Jesus possessed this gift when he multiplied a small ration of food to feed thousands.

Missionary: Ephesians 3:6–8—Called to other nations to share God's word.

Pastor: Ephesians 4:11—Similar to the gift of leadership, but is specific to leading a group of believers.

Prophecy (Ministry/Manifestation): Romans 12:6; 1 Corinthians 12:10; Ephesians 4:11—Given words from God to speak on future events or interpret current events.

Service: Romans 12:7—Serve in capacities to help others in whatever ways they are capable.

Teaching (Ministry): Romans 12:7; 1 Corinthians 12:28; Ephesians 4:11—Gifted to take God's word and instruct others in understanding and applying it to their lives.

Tongues (Manifestation): 1 Corinthians 12:10; 14:27–28—Speaking in a foreign or heavenly language to commune with God or communicate with others.

Interpretation of Tongues (Manifestation): 1 Corinthians 12:10; 14:27, 28—Interpret the language of those with the gifts of tongues to edify others.

Wisdom (Revelation): 1 Corinthians 12:8—Apply knowledge in practical ways to give insight into greater truths.

Teaching (Ministry): Romans 12:7; 1 Corinthians 12:28; Ephesians 4:11—Gifted to take God's word and instruct others in understanding and applying it to their lives.

Tongues (Manifestation): 1 Corinthians 12:10; 14:27–28—Speaking in a foreign or heavenly language to commune with God or communicate with others.

Interpretation of Tongues (Manifestation): 1 Corinthians 12:10; 14:27, 28—Interpret the language of those with the gifts of tongues to edify others.

Wisdom (Revelation): 1 Corinthians 12:8—Apply knowledge in practical ways to give insight into greater truths.

To identify your spiritual gifts, visit the following websites:

freeshapetest.com
mintools.com
giftstest.com

CHAPTER 15
ASSESSMENTS TO HELP DISCOVER YOUR PURPOSE

THE JAPANESE *IKIGAI** PHILOSOPHY CAN BE ROUGHLY DEFINED AS A method of finding one's purpose and motivation in life (from *iki*

---

meaning "life" and *gai* meaning "reason"). Because of its unique approach which is both idealistic and practical, personal and work-related, the *ikigai* concept and map is a useful tool for anyone seeking direction. It considers four spheres when approaching the question of what we should do with our lives (each sphere associated with a certain life focus or set of concerns):

- What You Love (Love)
- What the World Needs (Virtue)
- What You Can Be Paid For (Security)
- What You're Good At (Mastery)

Below is an explanation of what each of these spheres means in your life.

WHAT YOU LOVE

It will bring you joy if you do what you love. We are all seeking the things that money really can't buy—the intangible elements that make us happy. This can be the joy we feel when we are with those we love or the gratitude we feel when the medical test comes back negative, and when we know someone really loves us.

When we do what we love it stirs something within us that taps into our creative nature and being. It is something we would do all the time if we could. Doing what you love ties into purpose because purpose has everything to do with "Why" you do things. These are the things that drive you and that you are passionate about. Doing what you love puts you in alignment with what God created you to do. The world is filled with people doing things they don't love because they feel they must survive or make money. If more people were able to do what they love, they'd realize that doing what you love can make you more money than you ever thought possible.

WHAT THE WORLD NEEDS

This is connecting your love or passion for something with your natural gifts, talents and strength to meet a need that others may have. A good example of this is what recently happened in the mountains of North Carolina. After a recent hurricane, people of different passions and skills got together to help those who were left without homes, food, water, and power. When we can pair up our love and our skills with others' needs we will always be needed. This connection is what fulfills our purpose. We were created to meet a need. Once you identify your purpose and use it to fulfill a need, you have begun to discover the reason for your existence.

WHAT YOU CAN BE PAID FOR

This has everything to do with monetizing your purpose. The funny thing about living out your purpose vocationally is it doesn't even feel like working. Edison and Ford come to mind as examples. Both men loved what they did, tapped into their creative genius and worked endlessly, often without compensation, until their dreams manifested and they made lots of money. When we become experts in what we are passionate about, we can set our price and people will pay what we are asking. By mastering our purpose, we have set ourselves apart from others and are providing a much-needed service that people are willing to pay for.

WHAT YOU'RE GOOD AT

Doing what you're good at has so much to do with your gifts, talents, or strengths and ties back to what you love. When you love something, you're going to want to do more of it and better understand it. For example, if a boy grows up loving to watch cars race it is likely he may begin to study cars and how they operate. He may even take a class on auto mechanics. The more one feeds his passion, the better at it one becomes. Very few people are born with natural gifts, such as being able to paint or sing like a professional. If you lean into your natural gifts, talents and strengths and master your skill, you will naturally be sought after by others for your service.

As the initial diagram above shows, each sphere overlaps with others in ways that partially fill our life picture, though not all of it:

Mission (Love & Virtue):
What You Love & the World Needs

Vocation (Virtue & Security):
What the World Needs & You Can Be Paid For

Profession (Security & Mastery):
What You Can Be Paid For & You Are Good At

Passion (Mastery & Love):
What You Are Good At & Love

However, all of these spheres do overlap in the center, which is where we are truly aligned in all four spheres and our life is meaningful and in balance. By moving into the center of all four circles, we take actions that completely fulfill our *ikigai*, giving us a well-rounded sense of purpose and meaning.

To take an Ikigai assessment, visit:
ikigaitest.com

KOLBE A INDEX

The Kolbe A Index is a 36-question assessment that measures how a person takes action, both individually and when working with others. It assesses how we act cognitively (instinctively, why we do what we do) or purposely when we are being ourselves. The 36 questions examine four different modes of action, scoring answers on a scale of 1-10 in each mode to determine a person's method of operation. The four modes of action are:

1. **Fact Finder**: This mode measures how you gather and share information.
2. **Follow Through:** This mode measures how you organize information
3. **Quick Start**: This mode deals with how you deal with risks and uncertainty.
4. **Implementor:** This mode is how you handle space and tangibles.

The highest scores among these four action modes indicate a person's personal "method of operation," or the primary method they use to solve problems. When I took the test, my results were a three on Fact Finder, three on Follow Through, nine on Quick Start and a three in Implementor. With a low score as a Fact Finder, I don't need all the details in order to act, which is perfect for me as an entrepreneur and visionary: too much information overwhelms me. Being low on Follow Through means I adapt to information I get to make the best decision quickly, rather than overanalyzing or needing everything to be fixed in place.

My high score as a Quick Start means that I take in information, organize it in a way I can understand and then innovate to make the best decision I can. Finally, my low Implementor score means that I then have a broad idea of how my innovation could happen rather than planning all of the logistics—which is also perfectly in line with my entrepreneurial and visionary nature.

In a business or on a team, you must have a good overall balance of high scores in each category distributed across the entire team to be able to make wise, well-rounded decisions.

Personally, I look to Fact Finders to get information, then to high Follow Throughs to organize it and plan what to do. Finally, I look for strong Implementors to ensure it all gets done (and as a Quick Start, I can get momentum for the big picture through all the above without needing to do every step myself).

To take the Kolbe A Index assessment yourself, visit:
kolbe.com/kolbe-a-index

COLOR CODE

The Color Code test helps you determine not only *what* you do but *why* you do it, revealing your motives, needs and wants based on your personal hue. I've found it particularly helpful in understanding myself, connecting with others and building a cohesive team at work.

In the Color Code test, people are sorted into different colors or personality types (Red, Blue, White and Yellow) related to their personality and how they approach teamwork. Each color has its own traits and characteristics, as explained below:

RED

Reds are driven primarily by power and a need to be in control. They thrive on leadership, seek out positions of authority and are willing to sacrifice to get these positions. Productive and work-oriented, they only do tasks that interest them and try to avoid being forced to go along with others' priorities.

Similarly, Reds can be confrontational and tend more toward a sense of respect rather than open emotional connection. Their needs are primarily to be technically correct or "right", with concern for how they look to others. Likewise, their wants are to be challenged, have adventure, lead others and hide their insecurities. While Reds can be difficult to manage and may seem like "control freaks", they are often very productive on a team. To get the best from them, they need to have clear boundaries and neutral, unemotional communication based on objective facts.

BLUE

Primarily, blues look for intimacy and deep emotional bonds. They like helping others and looking for opportunities to make a positive impact. To have those meaningful relationships, they can be willing to sacrifice their own ambitions or success. They are very caring and altruistic, with a focus on understanding others and authentic connections.

Blues value emotional understanding over efficiency, and their moral compass guides their decisions. Being "good" and doing what's right is fulfilling to them, and their main needs are to be appreciated and understood as being ethical and having integrity. They want security and strong relationships where they can share and be vulnerable. Though blues can be sensitive or self-sacrificing, they are among the most trustworthy team members. To perform their best, they need to be sincerely appreciated and recognized, and given opportunities to connect with and help people.

WHITE

Peace and independence are what drives whites. They love harmony and having their space, avoiding confrontation as a way to maintain autonomy and balance in their lives. Whites are receptive and adaptable, going with the flow instead of imposing on others—but only if others treat them with kindness and respect.

Whites value a quiet sense of strength instead of loud, brute force; they resist control by others in a subtle but firm way. Although they may compromise to keep the peace, they know their own boundaries. Whites need to be allowed to go at their own pace, and to be shown kindness and respect—in fact, they often can't understand why anyone would act otherwise. They want freedom and contentment through following their own rhythm in life. Although whites can seem passive or too flexible at times, they do have their own resilience and drive. To draw it out of them, they need to be encouraged and treated gently, given respect and suggestions instead of outright demands.

YELLOW

Finally, what drives yellows is a sense of fun and play. They need social connection, thrive on excitement and attention and view life as a big party that is full of opportunities for entertainment and adventure. Socially oriented and energetic, yellows prioritize friendship and activities that will keep them engaged and excited.

In their interactions with others, yellows tend towards a free-flowing sense of play instead of intense focus. They lead with enthusiasm and physical connection, and they need consistent positive feedback in order to feel safe and secure. Getting social approval and attention is also key, as they have a strong desire to be praised. They look for opportunities to be in the middle of the room or the life of the party. Some yellows can seem nonchalant or restless, but they also have deep emotions below the surface. Giving yellows enough praise and time to socialize helps them stay engaged—this sense of understanding will bring out the best in them.

For a quick summary of all four color types—along with their motives, needs and wants—see the following table.

Color	Red	Blue	White	Yellow
Motives	Power	Intimacy	Peace	Fun
Needs	• To look good (technically)	• To be good (morally)	• To feel good (inside)	• To look good (socially)
	• To be right	• To be understood	• To be allowed their own space	• To be noticed
		• To be appreciated	• To be respected	• To be praised
			• Tolerance	• Approval from masses
Wants	• To hide insecurities	• To reveal insecurities	• To withhold insecurities	• To hide insecurities
	• Productivity	• Quality	• Kindness	• Happiness
	• Leadership	• Autonomy	• Independence	• Freedom
	• Challenging adventure	• Security	• Contentment	• Playful adventure

To take the Color Code Personality Test, visit:
colorcode.com/choose_personality_test

TRUE COLORS

The True Colors test also sorts into categories based on "color" of personality, with each person ending up either a blue, gold, green or orange. Specifically, the True Colors test tries to teach us how to deal with other personalities in a way that will best accentuate our own. Doing this results in a cohesive, productive workplace—so, in other words, this test is great to take with a team! Below are the common traits and patterns for each of the colors:

BLUE

Personalities
Taylor Swift • Oprah • Martin Luther King Jr. • Piglet from *Winnie the Pooh*

Traits
Optimistic • Accepting • Supportive • Caretaker • Enthusiastic • Passionate • Romantic • Peacemaker • Cooperative • Spiritual • People-oriented

Stressors
Conflict • Isolation • Rejection • Negativity • Being "used" • Apathy • Insincerity • Lack of acknowledgement or appreciation • Not being genuine • Not sharing • Saying "no"

Perception
Caring • Trusting • Giving benefit of doubt • Tirelessly working for a cause • Supportive • Genuinely interested in others

How Others May Perceive Them
Overly emotional • Naïve • Too committed • Smothering • Nosey

When Talking to a Blue
Acknowledge them • Be personable • Listen for feelings (talk privately) • Hear them out • "Feedback sandwich" strategy • Sincerity over sarcasm and teasing

If You Are a Blue
Try to read between the lines • Add "No" to your vocabulary • Speak up • Be more direct sometimes

- Try not to ramble and get to the point

Benefits in Teamwork
Enthusiasm • Mentoring • Team building • Support • Empathy

GOLD

Personalities
Hermione Granger • Martha Stewart • Mr. Rogers • George Washington • Rabbit from *Winnie the Pooh*

Traits
Prepared • Likes structure • Well-organized • Follows through • Detail-oriented • Loves to plan • Punctual • Procedural • Follows rules • Values tradition • Frugal

Stressors
Lack of follow-through • Not adhering to schedule or plans • Change • Unclear expectations • Not knowing where they fit or not belonging • Lack of consistency, leadership, master plan • Forced to neglect family time or traditions • Missing deadlines • Rule-breakers

Perception
Stable and dependable • Knowing what's best • Responsible • Goal-oriented • Punctual

How Others May Perceive Them
Rigid, stubborn • Judgmental • Bossy, controlling • Workaholic • Rigid about time

When Talking to a Gold
Communicate in writing • Don't interrupt • Be specific •

Closure • Stay on target (task, topic and time)
• Be consistent

If You Are a Gold
Have patience when others talk in different directions
• Be open-minded and consider other options • Be aware
of how hard you are driving yourself and others
• "Ease up" • Accept others' way of doing things if the
ultimate goal is the same

Benefits in Teamwork
Planning • Supervision • Rules or policies • Accuracy
• Organization and categorization

GREEN

Personalities
Spock • Abraham Lincoln • Steve Jobs • Benjamin
Franklin • Harry Potter • Owl from *Winnie the Pooh*

Traits
Innovative and inventive • Problem solver • "Why"
mentality • Calm, cool, collected • Intellectual
• Independent • Analytical and strategic
• Relationships are logical • Perfectionistic • Usually
tech-savvy

Stressors
Overly sensitive people • Lack of independent thinking
• Small talk • Mistakes or ineptitude in self or others •
Decisions made with no data • Redundancy or routine
• Red tape • Nothing new to look forward to, no variety
• Made to look incompetent

Perception
Knowledgeable • Confident •Innovative •Independent • Logical

How Others May Perceive Them
Intellectual snobs •Arrogant • Eccentric, weird • Anti-social • Heartless

When Talking to a Green
Give them time to think • Give independence • Stick to logic • Recognize their contributions and intelligence • Don't misinterpret their need for information

If You Are a Green
Ease up on the "whys" • Let others express their emotion • Learn to listen without "fixing" • Save the debate • Inform others when you are processing

Benefits in Teamwork
Information • Ideas • Creativity • Objective decision-making • Firmness • Critique and improvement

ORANGE

Personalities
Lucille Ball • Prince Harry • Captain Kirk • John F. Kennedy • Tigger from *Winnie the Pooh*

Traits
Energetic • Likes change • Playful • Master negotiator • Natural entertainer • Pushes boundaries • Fine with chaos • Makes things happen • Spontaneous and carefree • Thrives in non-structured environments

Stressors
Lack of freedom or choices, feeling trapped • Unable to use their skills • Forced to keep quiet or not participate • Insufficient attention • Waiting • Slow action • Indecisiveness • Routine • Lack of physical contact • Details, paperwork • Inactivity, restriction of physical movement

Perception
Straightforward • Keeps options open • Easy-going • Flexible Negotiator

How Others May Perceive Them
Rude, blunt, "no filter" • Irresponsible • Unserious • Ignores rules • Manipulative

When Talking to an Orange
Lighten up • Match their speed • Appreciate their flair • Be direct and to the point

If You Are an Orange
Be aware of how you are coming across • Give people time to process • Pause before committing

Benefits in Teamwork
Energy • Risk-taking • Entertainment • Laughs • Negotiation • Honesty

To take the True Colors test yourself, visit:
my-personality-test.com/true-colours

WORKING GENIUS

Originated by the Table Group, a company that offers consulting on organizational cultures, the Working Genius assessment is another great test to take with your team. The strength of the assessment is its simplicity. Cutting through many complex dynamics, it distills many different things at once and sorts people into the kinds of work that will help them thrive (and is one of very few tests to do so in this way).

The test helps identify a person's level of genius for six key attributes: Wonder, Invention, Discernment, Galvanizing, Enablement and Tenacity. These natural gifts or "Geniuses" are outlined below:

The Genius of Wonder: Pondering the possibility of greater potential and opportunity in a given situation.

The Genius of Invention: Creating original and novel ideas and solutions.

The Genius of Discernment: Intuitively and instinctively evaluating ideas and situations.

The Genius of Galvanizing: Rallying, inspiring and organizing others to take action.

The Genius of Enablement: Giving encouragement and assistance for an idea or project.

The Genius of Tenacity: Pushing projects or tasks to completion to achieve results.

These six Geniuses are further sorted into three groups: Ideation (Wonder, Invention), Activation (Wonder, Discernment) and Implementation (Enablement, Tenacity). This process helps create a Team Map, allowing leaders to sort team members by strengths and weaknesses (areas of Working Genius vs. Working Frustration) and make adjustments that lead to increased productivity and fulfillment.

While personality tests help us understand our own wiring

and work assessments look at our professional skills, the Working Genius assessment combines both to help an entire team understand how they can work together better on things like meetings, projects and hiring.

To learn more or to take the Working Genius assessment, visit:
workinggenius.com

THE WHY OF YOU (PRINT®)

Created by The Paul Hertz Group (PRINT®), The Why of You survey looks at human motivation and behavior to understand how and why people react the way they do, why they make certain choices, why they are attracted to certain things and why they perform better in certain situations compared to others. By getting these insights, the test hopes to help us increase our performance.

The Why of You reveals nine hidden drivers for our thoughts, feelings and actions (Unconscious Motivators), arguing that each person has two, one Major and one Minor. This system creates 72 different "prints" or profiles to help you understand your past actions and predict what you might do in the future.

In all, the goal of the survey is to help diminish the frequency of our Shadow behavior: negative actions that come from our Unconscious Motivators and take us away from our Best Self. Our Shadow is our automatic response to the stressors in our lives, but it may be more automatic for some people (while others might be closer to their Best Self automatically). A person's professional and personal environment plays a role, as does their level of self-awareness.

Knowing your Unconscious Motivators provides a foundation for increasing positive outcomes and reducing negative ones in all aspects of your life. We behave one way when our Unconscious Motivators are satisfied, because we act as our best selves. When they are unsatisfied, we can see it in our Shadow behaviors. For me personally, I can tell this happens when something triggers me and I become more reactionary.

The Why of You provides insight into why certain situations are appealing, why you gravitate to them and when you'll perform well. Knowing "why" accelerates your growth and transformation.

To take the PRINT® assessment, visit:
paulhertzgroup.com/what-is-print/

HUMAN DESIGN

Combining aspects of astrology, the I-Ching, Kabbalah and the chakra system, Human Design offers a personalized energetic blueprint called a Bodygraph that can help guide your life. The Bodygraph offers insights into decision-making and the purpose of our lives, as well as helping us improve our relationships, careers and overall sense of well-being.

Though Human Design is a complex assessment that takes time to understand, it begins with decoding the Bodygraph, which is determined by time of birth, day and location.*

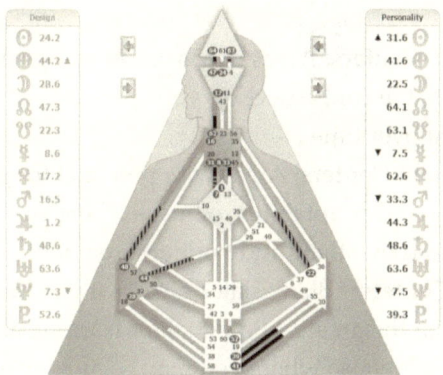

---

* Photo credit: Philip L. White, CC A-SA 3.0. https://commons.wikimedia.org/wiki/File:PLW-930am.png.

The Bodygraph has distinct sets of parts, as follows:

1. **Centers:** These nine geometric shapes correspond to your energy centers and different aspects of your being—namely the **Head (Inspiration), Ajna (Conceptualization), Throat (Communication), Self/G (Identity), Heart (Willpower), Sacral (Life Force), Solar Plexus (Emotions), Spleen (Intuition)** and **Root (Pressure).**
2. **Channels:** The lines connecting different centers are called channels. These represent the flow of energy between different aspects of your personality.
3. **Gates:** Within each center are various gates, representing different possible entries and exits (or paths) through each channel where energy can flow, which in turn represents different energies or themes in your life. There are 64 in total, mirroring the 64 hexagrams of the I-Ching.

Additionally, Centers can be **defined, undefined** or **open,** Channels can be **defined** or **undefined** and Gates can be **activate** or **inactive.** Each of these details also has unique significance:

1. **Defined Centers:** Areas of consistent energy and strength, the core aspects of your personality that are constant over time.
2. **Undefined Centers:** Areas with potential for growth, learning and adaptability, or areas where you are most influenced by others and your environment.
3. **Open Centers:** "Blank slate" areas with no defined gates and the greatest potential for learning and wisdom, but also where you may be most susceptible to conditioning and external influence.
4. **Defined Channels (Colored):** Fixed traits and consistent themes in your life which highlight natural

talents and areas where you can express yourself with confidence.

5. **Undefined Channels:** Opportunities for development and exploration, pointing to areas where you can gain wisdom through experiences and interactions with others.

6. **Activate Gates (Colored):** Specific energies that are active in your life, contributing to your unique expression and the lessons you are here to learn.

7. **Inactive Gates (White):** Represent potential areas for growth and exploration. These are aspects of your personality that may not be consistently expressed but can be developed or influenced by external factors.

In Human Design, the interplay of Centers, Channels and Gates leads each Bodygraph into one of five different Types of person: **Manifestors, Generators, Manifesting Generators, Projectors** and **Reflectors**. Each type has its own roles and traits, which are as follows:

1. **Manifestors**: Manifestors are initiators with the ability to make their ideas and visions a reality without needing to wait for external cues. Making up nine percent of the population of all humans, they make an impact by informing others of their intentions and paving the way for smoother interactions. Famous Manifestors include Frida Kahlo and Robert De Niro.

2. **Generators**: Generators are the builders and the doers. They possess a sustainable energy source energy that can lead to immense satisfaction and fulfillment when aligned with work they love. Making up 37 percent of the population, Generators often have careers that fully engage their skills and passions.

3. **Manifesting Generators**: A hybrid of the types above, Manifesting Generators are dynamic and efficient.

Making up 33 percent of the population, they can juggle multiple tasks and bring their visions to life with speed and effectiveness. In life, Manifesting Generators must follow their gut and communicate their plans to avoid resistance.

4. **Projectors**: Making up about 20 percent of the population, Projectors are guides and directors. They have a natural ability to understand systems and see the big picture, and their success depends on being recognized and invited to share insights.

5. **Reflectors**: Reflectors are the rarest type, making up only one percent of the population. These are the mirrors of society, reflecting the health and well-being of their community (or the lack of it). Reflectors' unique perspective allows them to offer objective insights, but also means they need more time to process their experiences before making decisions.

Each Type has its own **Strategy**, or method of achieving our best outcomes through interactions with others:

- **Generators and Manifesting Generators**: Waiting to respond, trusting the gut.
- **Manifestors**: Initiating action and informing others to reduce resistance.
- **Projectors**: Waiting for invitations to share insights.
- **Reflectors**: Waiting for a full lunar cycle before a significant decision.

All of the above combine in even greater detail to define a person's **Authority** (seven options related to Centers and affecting decision-making), **Circuitry** (shape of energy flowing through Gates and Channels) and **Profile** (12 options depending on our Circuitry and affecting our conscious and unconscious sides). Since this system is so involved, it can take more time to process, but it can also result in rich insights about our lives.

To explore your own Human Design Bodygraph, visit:
myhumandesign.com

ELEMENTS TEST

The Elements test is a fun one! Designed for kids (and encouraging you to take the test as your 15-year-old self), it looks at the fundamental energies behind our energy and leadership qualities. Through the test, we are sorted into five elemental archetypes: **Wood, Fire, Water, Earth** and **Gold**. These relate to various traits and tendencies, as explained below:

- **Fire**: Celebration, passion, optimism, playfulness, spontaneity, creativity and relaxation, willpower, leadership. Those who align with Fire energy are action-oriented, adventurous and passionate.
- **Earth**: Harmony, collaboration, community, empathy, trust, cooperation, agreement, patience, discipline, stability. Those who align with Earth are practical, reliable and grounded.
- **Water**: Intuition, insight, meaning, patience, privacy, introspection, dignity, peace, emotional intelligence, adaptability. Water-oriented people are nurturing, empathetic and flexible.
- **Wood**: Freedom, movement, purpose, drive, goals, independence, competition, choice. Those aligned with Wood are outgoing, adventurous, expansive and courageous.
- **Gold**: Grace, beauty, excellence, order, routine, accuracy, justice, predictability. Gold types tend to be organized, calm, resourceful and reserved.

By examining your fundamental energies, the Elements Test provides:

- **Enhanced Self-Awareness**: Understanding of core strengths and areas for improvement.
- **Better Interpersonal Skills**: How to interact with others by recognizing their elemental energies.
- **More Balanced Leadership**: Leading holistically by integrating all five elements.
- **Personal and Professional Growth**: Creating well-rounded teams by balancing elemental energies for better collaboration.
- **Fulfillment**: Finding harmony by balancing all of these aspects.

To take the Elements test, visit:
tournesolkids.org/assessment

DISC® ASSESSMENT

The DiSC® assessment is designed to harmonize your workplace and issued by more than a million people each year to improve teamwork, communication and productivity at work. The profiles found in this test—sorted as D, i, S and C—provide the knowledge your team needs to understand itself and communicate with itself. As described in the assessment itself, each category comes with its own traits:

- **(D)ominance**: Confident personalities, emphasis on bottom-line results.
- **(i)nspiring**: Open personalities, emphasis on influence, persuasion and relationships.
- **(S)upportive**: Dependable personalities, emphasis on cooperation and sincerity.

- **(C)onscientiousness:** Detail-oriented personalities, emphasis on quality, accuracy, expertise and competency.

The assessment evaluates a person's priorities to give more nuance and feedback about their individual personalities, but it is also valuable at scale as well, for organizations to understand how to build better teams, improve communication, approach sales and more. Much like other workplace assessments, the test helps us understand how to achieve balance between ourselves and others who display the four traits mentioned above.

To take the DiSC ® *assessment, visit:*
thediscpersonalitytest.com

ENNEAGRAM

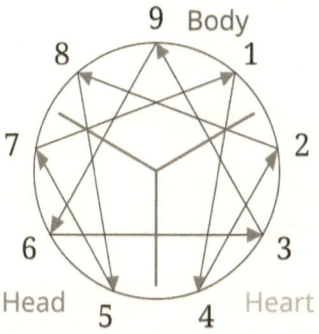

Put simply, the Enneagram* is a wheel of nine distinct personality types, with each number representing one type. While we have parts of all nine points in our personality, the Enneagram sorts us into a **Dominant Type** which orients us toward the

---

* Photo credit: DomenicoL76. CC0 1.0. https://commons.wikimedia.org/wiki/File:Enneagram_Type.svg.

world. Our Dominant Type can be determined by a question-naire, resulting in one of nine roles in the world related to each number:

The Reformer (1):
Principled, purposeful, self-controlled, perfectionistic.

The Helper (2):
Generous, demonstrative, people-pleasing, possessive.

The Achiever (3):
Adaptable, excelling, driven, image-conscious.

The Individualist (4):
Expressive, dramatic, self-absorbed, temperamental.

The Investigator (5):
Perceptive, innovative, secretive, isolated.

The Loyalist (6):
Engaging, responsible, anxious, suspicious.

The Enthusiast (7):
Spontaneous, versatile, acquisitive, scattered.

The Challenger (8):
Self-confident, decisive, willful, confrontational.

The Peacemaker (9):
Receptive, reassuring, complacent, resigned.

Within the wheel, the Enneagram also has a three-by-three set of **Centers: Instinctive (8-9), Feeling (2-4)** and **Thinking (5-7)** (related to **the body, the heart and the mind)**. The personalities in each Center are related to certain sets of unconscious, lifelong emotions we struggle with at our core. For Instinctives, these emotions are *Anger* and *Rage*; for the Feeling Center, the emotion is *Shame*; and for the Thinking Center, the emotion is *Fear*.

Additionally, our Dominant Type also forms one or two **Wings** (connections across the wheel) with other numbers we most closely relate to. The combination of our Dominant Type and Wings creates a set of patterns, strategies, defenses and obstacles to overcome throughout our lives. These patterns represent the archetypal internal structures and struggles of different personalities, but are made more complicated by our personality's **Level of Integration (Growth) or Disintegration (Stress)** in the face of those challenges.

These Levels can be thought of as the "path" we take around the Enneagram when under pressure or strain, depending on if our sense of self is integrating or disintegrating. Rather than go around the circle as we change, we take a jagged, star-shaped path through all the different points of personality in either a healthy or unhealthy direction. For all different Dominant Types, there are only a few main paths in either direction:

Direction of Integration (Growth):
1-7-5-8-2-4-1, 9-3-6-9

Direction of Disintegration (Stress):
1-4-2-8-5-7-1, 9-6-3-9

To understand these numbers, it's important to know that our Level of Development can be **Healthy (Levels 1-3)**, **Average (Levels 4-6)** or **Unhealthy (Levels 7-9)** at any given time. In the Disintegration number line, for example, the numbers mean that an average to unhealthy One (first number) under stress will eventually shift into the behaviors of an average to unhealthy Four (second number) and so on, getting further and further away from their nature, while the opposite is true of the Integration line (the lines between 3, 6 and 9 represents another pattern for personalities in that set).

Though the Enneagram is complex (and still has additional details to uncover), it is a comprehensive test that shows both who you are and who you are susceptible to becoming.

To take the Enneagram test for yourself, visit:
enneagramtest.com

ANIMAL TEMPERAMENT TEST

Finally, the Animal Temperament Test is similar to the Temperament Test mentioned in Chapter 10. The assessment sorts us according to "temperaments" that align with four animal types: **Lion, Otter, Golden Retriever** and **Beaver** (similar to Choleric, Sanguine, Phlegmatic and Melancholy, which were mentioned earlier.) These types behave as follows:

LION (CHOLERIC)

Decisive leaders and bosses (or at least they think they are!), these bottom-line folks are observers who love to solve problems. Confident, self-reliant and take-charge types, these people can be aggressive and dominating, which can be a challenge. It may be no surprise that many entrepreneurs are Lions!

Natural Strengths and Weaknesses:
Decisive • Takes charge • Impatient • Can be insensitive to the feelings of others • Goal-oriented • Takes initiative • Blunt • Risk-taker • Achievement driven • Self-starter • Poor listener • Fears inactivity, relaxation • Gets results • Persistent • Impulsive • Persistent • Independent • Quickly bored by routine or mechanics • Demanding • Competitive • May "run over" others who are slower to act or speak • May view projects more important than

people • Enjoys challenges, variety and change • Driven to complete projects quickly and effectively

Basic Disposition:
Fast-paced, task-oriented.

Motivated By:
Results; challenge, action, power and credit for achievement.

Time Management:
Focused on *now* instead of the distant future. They get a lot more done in a lot less time than their peers. Hate wasting time; and like to get to the point.

Communication Style:
Great at initiating communication, but not good at listening (one way communicator).

Decision-Making:
Impulsive, makes quick decisions with a goal or end result in mind. Results-focused and needs very few facts to make a decision.

In Pressure or Tense Situations:
The Lion takes command and becomes autocratic.

Greatest Needs:
The Lion needs to see results, experience variety, and face new challenges. He needs to solve problems and wants direct answers.

Desires:
Freedom, authority, variety, difficult assignments, opportunity for advancement.

OTTER (SANGUINE)

Otters are excitable, fun seeking, cheerleader types who love to talk! They're great at motivating others and need to be in an environment where they can talk and have a vote on major decisions. The otters' outgoing nature makes them great networkers —they usually know a lot of people who know a lot of people. They can be very loving and encouraging unless under pressure, when they tend to use their verbal skills to attack. They have a strong desire to be liked and enjoy being the center of attention. They are often very attentive to style, clothes, and flash. Otters are the life of any party; and most people really enjoy being around them.

Natural Strengths and Weaknesses:
Enthusiastic • Unrealistic • Optimistic • Not detail-oriented • Good Communicator • Disorganized • Emotional and Passionate • Impulsive • Motivational and Inspirational • Listens to feelings above logic • Outgoing • Reactive • Personal • Can be too talkative • Dramatic • Excitable • Fun-loving

Basic Disposition: Fast-paced. People-oriented.

Motivated By: Recognition and approval of others.

Time Management: Focused on the future, with a tendency to rush to the next exciting thing.

Communication Style: Enthusiastic and stimulating, often one-way; but can inspire and motivate others.

Decision-Making: Intuitive and fast. Makes lots of "right calls" and lots of wrong ones.

In Pressure or Tense Situations: *Attack!* Can be more concerned about their popularity than about achieving tangible results.

Greatest Needs: Social activities and recognition, activities that are fun and freedom from details.

Desires: Prestige, friendly relationships, opportunity to help and motivate others and opportunities to verbally share their ideas.

GOLDEN RETRIEVER (PHLEGMATIC)

These people can be described with one word: *loyal*. They're so loyal, in fact, that they can absorb the most emotional pain and punishment in a relationship and still stay committed. They are great listeners, incredibly empathetic and warm encouragers. However, they tend to be such pleasers that they can have great difficulty being assertive when necessary in certain situations or relationships.

Natural Strengths and Weaknesses:
Patient • Indecisive • Easy-going • Too accommodating • May sacrifice results for harmony • Team player • Stable • Slow to initiate • Empathetic • Avoids confrontation even when needed • Compassionate • Can hold grudges and remember hurts • Sensitive to others' feelings • Puts people above projectsTremendously loyal • Fears change • Dependable • Reliable • Supportive • Agreeable

Basic Disposition:
Slow-paced, people-oriented.

Motivated By:
Desire for good relationships and appreciation of others.

Time Management:
Focused on the present and devote lots of time to helping others and building relationships.

Communication Style:
Two-way communicator; great listener and provides empathetic response.

Decision-Making:
Makes decisions more slowly, wants input from others and often yields to the input.

In Pressure or Tense Situations:
Gives in to the opinions, ideas and wishes of others. Often too tolerant.

Greatest Needs:
Security; gradual change and time to adjust to it; an environment free of conflict.

Desires:
Quality relationships; security; consistent known environment; a relaxed and friendly environment; freedom to work at own pace.

BEAVER (MELANCHOLY)

Beavers have a strong need to do things right and by the book. In fact, they are the kind of people who actually read instruction manuals. They are great at providing quality control in an office, and will provide quality control in any situation or field that demands accuracy, such as accounting, engineering, etc. Because rules, consistency and high standards are so important to beavers, they are often frustrated with others who do not share these same characteristics. Their strong need for maintaining high (and oftentimes unrealistic) standards can short-circuit their ability to express warmth in a relationship.

Natural Strengths and Weaknesses:
Accurate • Too hard on self • Analytical • Too critical of others • Detail-oriented • Perfectionist • Thoroughness • Over-cautious • Industrious • Orderly • Won't make decisions without "all" the facts • Too picky • Overly sensitive • Methodical and exhaustive • High standards • Intuitive • Controlled

Basic Disposition:
Slow-paced, task-oriented.

Motivated By:
The desire to be right and to maintain a level of quality.

Time Management:
Tend to work slowly to make sure they are accurate.

Communication Style:
Good listeners who communicate details and are usually diplomatic.

Decision-Making:
Avoids making decisions; needs lots of information before they will make a decision.

In Pressure or Tense Situations:
Tries to avoid pressure or tense situations. They can ignore deadlines.

Greatest Needs:
Security, gradual change and time to adjust to it.

Desires:
Clearly defined tasks, stability, security, low risk and tasks that require precision and planning.

In all, this test puts a fun spin on an old classic with its animal personalities, a feature that makes more engaging and easier to interpret.

To take the Animal Temperament assessment, visit:
focusonthefamily.com/marriage/4-animals-personality-test

CHAPTER 16
CREATING
A PURPOSE STATEMENT

IF YOU ENTER THE BREAK ROOM OF NEARLY ANY COMPANY, YOU MAY see a poster with the words "Mission Statement." A mission statement is a short blurb that explains why the company does what they do. Rarely have I seen a company use the words "Purpose Statement."

I recently became aware of the importance of purpose statements. The question of purpose addresses the "why" of what we do. It is the heart of what we are most passionate about. I better understood myself when I learned about my gifts, talents, personality, spiritual gifts, temperaments, passions and love language. From those came my purpose, which I turned into a purpose statement that I recite daily. It is my GPS to guide me in what I do and how I ought to act. This is my purpose statement:

I will love the Lord my God with all my heart, soul, mind and body, and love others as myself. This will be reflected in my thoughts, words and actions each day.

Love is what drives me. If God is love and every part of me is loving Him, myself and others, then I am living out my purpose. My purpose statement was a work in progress while I sought to understand what my purpose was. Once I did, I needed a statement that described how I was to live it each day. I realized that, after many years of "wandering through the desert," helplessly searching for what I was to do with my life, I had an obligation to live it fully.

I chose to speak about loving God because love drives everything I do. In order to live my purpose, I needed to better understand how to love. I had to first go to the true source of love: God, our Creator. I had to learn how to love Him. He would teach me how to love myself and others. When my heart's desires are met through Him, I won't seek to meet those needs in unhealthy and destructive ways. My love for Him had to be reflected not only in my heart, but in my soul, mind and body— in everything I am. The second part of my purpose statement is about how that love is reflected. First Corinthians 13 best illustrates this:

If I speak in the tongues of men or of angels, but do not have love, I am only a resounding gong or a clanging cymbal. If I have the gift of prophecy and can fathom all mysteries and all knowledge, and if I have a faith that can move mountains, but do not have love, I am nothing. If I give all I possess to the poor and give over my body to hardship that I may boast, but do not have love, I gain nothing.

Love is patient, love is kind. It does not envy, it does not boast, it is not proud. It does not dishonor others, it is not self-seeking, it is not easily angered, it keeps no record of wrongs. Love does not delight in evil but rejoices with the truth. It always protects, always trusts, always hopes, always perseveres.

Love never fails. But where there are prophecies, they will cease; where there are tongues, they will be stilled; where there is knowledge, it will pass away. For we know in part and we prophesy in part, but when completeness comes, what is in part disappears. When I was a child, I talked like a child, I thought like a child, I reasoned like a child. When I became a man, I put the ways of childhood behind me. For now we see only a reflection as in a mirror; then we shall see face to face. Now I know in part; then I shall know fully, even as I am fully known.

And now these three remain: faith, hope and love. But the greatest of these is love.

—New International Version, I Corinthians 13

I recognized that my purpose in this life is to love, not only in word, but in deed. That love first originates in my heart, and is reinforced in my love for others, illustrated by my words and actions. As the old Beatles song says, "all you need is love." There is definite truth to that.

"Above all, love each other deeply, because love covers over a multitude of sins."

—New International Version, 1 Peter 4:8

When you sit down to develop your purpose statement, recognize there is no rush. I would recommend you put as much thought and prayer into this endeavor as needed. Remember that this will be your GPS, so you want to make sure it accurately reflects your heart.

Purpose is the "heart" of who you are—it is what drives and motivates you. In order to discover the jewel buried inside, you must dig a little. You must ask a lot of questions, not only to yourself, but to those who know you, who have your best interest at heart. Avoid negative and discouraging people—even friends and family members—because they might not want the best for you. The passion exercise and strengths assessment will be very helpful for the development of your purpose statement.

Your purpose will primarily consist of whatever you are good at and passionate about. For example, Martin Luther King Jr.'s gifts were his passion for civil rights and his ability to inspire people through his speeches. He used his gifts—his passion—to live out his purpose. Try to keep it down to one or two sentences, then commit it to memory. Once you come up with something that feels right, doors of opportunity will open. You will find that you are doing less of what you don't want, and more of what you do want to do. You will see how to better use your time and energy to serve others.

CHAPTER 17
CREATING A VISION STATEMENT

THE NEXT STEP, AFTER DEVELOPING YOUR PURPOSE STATEMENT, IS TO develop a vision statement. It is important to do it in this order because, to know where you're going, you must first know *why* you're going. Alice faced this challenge in *Alice's Adventures in Wonderland* by Lewis Carroll:

> *Alice asked the Cheshire Cat, who was sitting in a tree, "What road do I take?"*
> *The cat asked, "Where do you want to go?"*
> *"I don't know," Alice answered.*
> *'Then," said the cat, "it really doesn't matter, does it?"*

Many people have a destination, but they don't know why they are going there. When I say I am going to the store, the reason is that I need groceries. If I say I am going to the gas station, it usually means I need to buy gas. Most of us have a reason to set out for a destination. It may be somewhat generic, like when I got in the car two summers ago with my kids and said, "We are heading west to California!" Of course, they asked me why, and I told them, "Because we want to!" It was something we had always wanted to do, and we had the best time.

When you decide where you want to go and why you want to go, you put the coordinates into your GPS, which finds the best route for you to take. The final destination is the vision. The reason for wanting to go is the purpose.

The purpose statement is the "heart" of why you want to do it; the vision statement is the "eyes" that see the path laid out before you, and the mission statement are the "legs" you use to actually get you there.

Once again, here is my purpose statement:

I will love the Lord my God with all my heart, soul, mind and body, and love others as myself. This will be reflected in my thoughts, words and actions each and every day.

This was my "why." I then had to figure out how I was going to get there and what my destination was. Love drives me, and helping others is what I do. I looked at what inspired me when I was helping others. It started years ago when God laid this course on my heart. Life experiences and lessons have expanded this course to where it is today. It all began when I decided to help people understand their purpose in life and how they were uniquely created by God. Once I saw people's eyes open, I began to see what my vision was:

To see people living out their purpose in life and loving and serving one another with their gifts and talents.

My vision was directly linked to my purpose—using my gifts and talents to help others discover their gifts and talents, and ultimately their own purpose. When we use our gifts and talents in line with our purpose, we will reach our destination—a life we are proud of in which we bless many by our actions. By doing that, we live complete lives that will leave a true and lasting legacy.

The process for developing your own vision statement is not that much different than the process for developing your purpose statement. It is a little easier since you now have your purpose statement, which is your "why." Use this as your starting point in figuring out where you want to go.

For example, if a person's passion and purpose is to help educate kids in reading, his or her vision statement might be something like this:

My vision is to provide young kids with an increased opportunity to read. I will do this by volunteering at local schools and encouraging children to seek advanced learning in college. I will encourage them to always keep dreaming and believing that all things are possible.

It is important that vision statements provide the direction of how you're going to reach your ultimate goal. It does not have to be detailed. Your ultimate goal doesn't need to be specific, but it must point you in the right direction.

Your purpose is passion and fuel. Your vision is what you believe you will accomplish with your purpose. The goals, steps and tasks break down the vision into manageable steps.

CHAPTER 18
CREATING A MISSION STATEMENT

As I STATED BEFORE, A MISSION STATEMENT IS WHAT YOU TYPICALLY see posted in a company break room. It is important to have your purpose statement because that is your "why." It is equally important to have your vision statement because that is "where" you're going. It is important to have your mission statement because it tells you "how" you're going to get there. It should also be memorized and recited daily. From the mission statement you can develop goals and strategic plans for how you are going to accomplish those goals, breaking them down further into steps and tasks. Here is my mission statement:

I will daily serve others with my gifts, passions and talents to draw them closer to Christ so that He may reveal His purpose and will for their lives. I will do this by being an encourager, teacher and mentor.

When I looked at what my gifts and talents were, and recognized my love and passion for teaching, encouraging and mentoring others, it became clear what my mission statement was going to say, or more importantly, *do*. None of this would be possible without my relationship with God. It is only through what He has taught me that I was inspired to share what I learned. I can instruct, teach, encourage and mentor; however, I believe it is only God who can reveal. One of my favorite verses illustrates this:

> *I keep asking that the God of our Lord Jesus Christ, the glorious Father, may give you the Spirit of wisdom and revelation, so that you may know him better. I pray that the eyes of your heart may be enlightened in order that you may know the hope to which he has called you, the riches of his glorious inheritance in his holy people, and his incomparably great power for us who believe. That power is the same as the mighty strength.*
> —New International Version, Ephesians 1:17–19

God desires to reveal His purpose for us. If he doesn't, why then would He create us? Use your purpose and vision statements as guides to help you develop your own mission statement. Detail in the statement some specifics as to what you want to accomplish. Remember, it is the "legs" of how you're going to get there. Based on the previous example about helping kids learn to read, their mission statement might read something like this:

I will commit to reading with a group of kids at my local elementary school one hour a week, and encourage them to read throughout the week and share with me what they have read.

Purpose, vision and mission statements set the stage. You must follow up with setting annual, quarterly, monthly and weekly goals that all focus back to your purpose. Each day, you must review these goals and set tasks for the day to help you accomplish those goals. Review your goals often. I also encourage you to share your intentions with a good friend who can keep you accountable.

CHAPTER 19
PUTTING IT ALL TOGETHER

As we near the end of our journey, it is time to lay all the pieces of the puzzle down and see what the picture looks like. As you have ventured through this book and completed all the assessments, quizzes and tests to see what makes you uniquely you, you may have discovered that you are already living out your purpose. I encourage you to keep doing what you love. Some of you may realize that what you're doing is nowhere near your purpose. I encourage you to seek what brings you passion and lines up with your strengths, gifts, talents, temperament and personality.

You may not know what the rest of your life will look like, but you will be on the right path to creating the life you have always dreamed of. Ken Robinson PhD, in his book, *The Element: How Finding Your Passion Changes Everything*, wrote, "The element is the place where the things we love to do and the things we are good at come together."

STRENGTHS

I have used the CliftonStrengths Assessment to better understand my strengths. Other options are the Strong Interest Inventory® or the High5 Strengths Test Methodology and Approach. When you learn what you are good at, you can become an expert in your area of interest or career. The Beatles were very good musicians and combined their talent with their passion to perform. They were a huge hit. Not everyone can be The Beatles, but the steps they took are no different than the steps the rest of us must take. If we learn what we are good at—music, art, math, science, public speaking or connecting with people—we can perfect that strength and focus it into something we love.

GIFTS

The abilities given to us at birth develop as we grow. We can use these abilities to bless and serve others. They differentiate us from others, and help us fulfill our purpose. Someone may have the gift of compassion or encouragement. Someone may have a gift for mechanical work or problem solving. Using our gifts is vital to fulfilling our purpose.

TALENTS

These could be music or language or other things we are generally good at. These may be related to gifts, but not necessarily, as talents can be learned and developed. When we use our talents and also improve on them, we can be of better service to others.

SPIRITUAL GIFTS

Discovering our spiritual gifts allows us to tap into the soul aspect of our purpose as it relates to service. It allows us to understand each person's spiritual uniqueness. We may each have multiple spiritual gifts, but they usually complement each other.

PASSIONS

These are the aspects of our lives that "light our fire," like working with kids, or creating art or music. These are things we are just drawn to; we cannot live without them. Our passions fuel us and energize us. They are the important "whys" in our lives.

LOVE LANGUAGE

Our love language represents how we prefer to give and receive love. This is not necessarily romantic love, but all expressions of love toward others. This is important in any relationship, especially as it pertains to expectations. Often we get frustrated in relationships because we provide expressions of love that meet our needs, and when others don't respond as we expected, we are disappointed. For example, my two love languages, in order, are physical touch and quality time. If I use touch to try to meet someone's needs, but their love language is acts of service, my effort wouldn't have as strong an effect. It is important to know our love language and, equally important, know the love languages of those we care about so we can better relate to them.

TEMPERAMENT

There are four types of temperament: sanguine (otter), phlegmatic (golden retriever), choleric (lion), and melancholy (beaver). Each of us may possess a variety of temperaments. Temperament may be aligned to life's work; leaders are typically high choleric; counselors or those in the service fields are typically phlegmatic; accountants, engineers and detail-oriented folks are typically melancholic; politicians and sales people are sanguines. There is some direct correlation with the Myers-Briggs Type Indicator® as it relates to introversion and extroversion. Typically, sanguines and cholerics are extroverts and phlegmatics and melancholies are introverts. For example, I am a phlegmatic, my second is choleric and my third is sanguine. I can come across as extroverted, but I gain my energy from spending time with myself.

PERSONALITY TYPE

Based on the Myers-Briggs Type Indicator®, personality types are variations of the following: how we focus (extrovert versus introvert), how we make decisions (thinking versus feeling), how we take in information (sensing versus intuition) and how we choose to live our outer lives (judging versus perceiving). Knowing our type can help us have a better understanding of who we are, how we relate and how we think and process. To quote Socrates, "To know thyself is the beginning of wisdom."

PERSONALITY STYLE

Our personality is the distinctive pattern of our psychological functioning: the combination of how we think, feel and behave that makes us who we are. The New Personality Self-Portrait 25 delineates 14 personality styles which, in each person's unique combination, shape the manner in which we endeavor to lead a productive and satisfying life, adapt to change and solve problems. This is important because it gives us insight as to why we react the way we do. It also gives us insight into how some of our personality styles may lead us toward negative tendencies.

CHAPTER 20
NOW THAT YOU KNOW, WHAT DO YOU DO?

HOPEFULLY, AFTER YOU FINISH READING THIS BOOK, YOU WILL GO back and reread certain sections and start to apply what you have learned. If you keep your purpose as your main focus, you will see opportunity after opportunity that will confirm you are on the right path. In the poem "The Road Not Taken" by Robert Frost, he writes:

> *Two roads diverged in a wood, and I—*
> *I took the one less traveled by,*
> *and that has made all the difference.*

Often it is easier to follow the path others are taking, but that won't necessarily lead you where you want to go. The path less traveled may seem uncertain, but challenges are there to make you stronger, to make you worthy of what you were created for. Another quote, this one by Steven Covey, comes to mind: "To learn and not to do is really not to learn. To know and not to do is really not to know."

The greatest gift God gave us was the power of choice. He said if we seek Him, we will find Him. His greatest desire is for us to seek Him. He wants to reveal Himself to His children so that He can bless us. He has a special plan for using each of us, and this is why He has gifted each of us with unique strengths. Once you know what these are, you must use them in the service of others.

> *"For even the Son of man did not come to be served, but to serve, and to give your life as a ransom for many."*
> —New International Version, Mark 10:45

Jesus lived this when He washed his disciples' feet:

> *Jesus knew that the Father had put all things under his power, and that he had come from God and was returning to God; so he got up from the meal, took off his outer clothing, and wrapped a towel around his waist. After that, he poured water into a basin and began to wash his disciples' feet, drying them with the towel that was wrapped around him. He came to Simon Peter, who said to him, "Lord, are you going to wash my feet?"*
>
> *Jesus replied, "You do not realize now what I am doing, but later you will understand."*
>
> *"No," said Peter, "you shall never wash my feet."*
>
> *Jesus answered, "Unless I wash you, you have no part with me."*
>
> *"Then, Lord," Simon Peter replied, "not just my feet but my hands and my head as well!"*
>
> *Jesus answered, "Those who have had a bath need only to wash their feet; their whole body is clean. And you are clean, though not every one of you." For he knew who was going to betray him, and that was why he said not every one was clean.*
>
> *When he had finished washing their feet, he put on his clothes and returned to his place. "Do you understand what I have done for you?" he asked them. "You call me 'Teacher' and 'Lord,' and rightly so, for that is what I am. Now that I, your Lord and Teacher, have washed your feet, you also should wash one another's feet. I have set you an example that you should do*

as I have done for you. Very truly I tell you, no servant is greater than his master, nor is a messenger greater than the one who sent him. Now that you know these things, you will be blessed if you do them."
—New International Version, John 13:3–17

The great reward in finding your purpose is not only the discovery, but in the ability to bless others. Everything has been created for a purpose, and that purpose can only be properly revealed for its use in service.

CHAPTER 21
LEAVING A LEGACY

THERE ARE MANY WAYS TO BE REMEMBERED. OBITUARIES ONLY WORK if people actually read them. We can stroll through a cemetery and get even shorter views of people's lives, but we usually learn only when they were born and when they died.

So, how do we leave our mark? Our legacy is how we love others, serve them and bless them. The truest mark of our lives is how others remember us and share those memories. A successful life is one that lives on in others. Legacy represents the culmination of our life's work and calling—the investment we made in people and the things we believed in. When we serve others, our legacy will live on through them.

It is great to have a building named after you to commemorate your life, but a more indelible tribute is to have your character carry on through others. Leaving a legacy doesn't start the day you find out you have one year to live. It starts when you live your life to love and serve others. That starts today. The sooner we discover that, the better.

David Brainerd was an American missionary to the Native Americans in the 1700s. He only lived to the age of 28, when died suddenly. He is greatly remembered for his sacrifice and service. He impacted generations with his service. His legacy will always be his sacrifice and service to others.

Legacy is not what we get, it's what we give. The daily choices we make will define our character and establish our legacy. History speaks favorably and unfavorably of many legacies. As powerful as he was, Hitler will always be viewed in a negative light. His negative legacy is the result of his character as a dictator and tyrant. Lincoln will always be remembered favorably for his courage under fire to free the slaves. Edison will be remembered for overcoming all odds to bring light to a dark world. Henry Ford will be remembered for bringing automobiles to the common man.

Once we are gone, we can't change how people will see us. So, always be true to yourself and seek to love and serve those around you. Most importantly, choose to use your purpose, talents, and gifts to bless others.

Be proactive and write your epitaph before your day of departure arrives. Wouldn't you rather have a say in what is written about you, since it is your life they are talking about? By writing down your thoughts, you set a standard for yourself that is worthy of the legacy you will leave. We don't know the hour or the day of our demise, so we should keep busy living life and preparing for the hereafter.

CONCLUSION

Thank you so much for walking with me on this journey. Ancient Chinese philosophy, the *Tao Te Ching*, reminds us that a journey of a thousand miles begins with a single step. You have taken the most important step. You have blessed me by picking up this book. You have also blessed me by finishing it. In some respects, this book was a fulfillment of my own purpose—to teach others how to find their purpose.

My hope is that you now have a clearer sense of what you were created to do. The challenge now is to go out and do it. Knowledge without action is no better than having no knowledge at all. Our growth in life comes only as we apply the things we have learned. We make corrections along the way until we arrive at our destination, and in our case, our destiny. I close with these two passages from scripture. The first is the parable of the talents:

> *Again, it will be like a man going on a journey, who called his servants and entrusted his wealth to them. To one he gave five bags of gold, to another two bags, and to another one bag, each according to his ability. Then he went on his journey. The man who had received five bags of gold went at once and put his*

money to work and gained five bags more. So also, the one with two bags of gold gained two more. But the man who had received one bag went off, dug a hole in the ground and hid his master's money.

After a long time the master of those servants returned and settled accounts with them. The man who had received five bags of gold brought the other five. 'Master,' he said, 'you entrusted me with five bags of gold. See, I have gained five more.'

His master replied, 'Well done, good and faithful servant! You have been faithful with a few things; I will put you in charge of many things. Come and share your master's happiness!'

The man with two bags of gold also came. 'Master,' he said, 'you entrusted me with two bags of gold; see, I have gained two more.'

His master replied, 'Well done, good and faithful servant! You have been faithful with a few things; I will put you in charge of many things. Come and share your master's happiness!'

Then the man who had received one bag of gold came. 'Master,' he said, 'I knew that you are a hard man, harvesting where you have not sown and gathering where you have not scattered seed. So I was afraid and went out and hid your gold in the ground. See, here is what belongs to you.'

His master replied, 'You wicked, lazy servant! So you knew that I harvest where I have not sown and gather where I have not scattered seed? Well then, you should have put my money on deposit with the bankers, so that when I returned I would have received it back with interest.

'So take the bag of gold from him and give it to the one who has ten bags. For whoever has will be given more, and they will have an abundance. Whoever does not have, even what they have will be taken from them.

—New International Version, Matthew 25:14–29

We are all given talents and gifts, and the expectation is we will use them so they can multiply. If we don't, they will be taken away. We have an opportunity to recognize all that God has given to us and to use it as a blessing to others and, by default, to ourselves.

The second passage I would like to share is the apostle Paul speaking near the end of his life about his calling. Many of us are like Paul. He was a very learned man set on a course living out what he thought was his purpose—to persecute the new converts of Christianity. Sometimes God intervenes in miraculous ways and redirects our paths. He did with Paul on the road to Damascus, and Paul was miraculously converted. His newfound purpose revolutionized the history of the Christian church. This was his closing statement on his life:

> *For I am already being poured out like a drink offering, and the time for departure is near. I have fought the good fight, I have finished the race, I have kept the faith. Now there is in store for me the crown of righteousness, which the Lord, the righteous judge will award to me on that day—and not only to me but also to all who have long for his appearing.*
> —New International Version, 2 Timothy 4:6–8

Paul knew his purpose, and even though he sacrificed much, it was all for his own gain. He knew what he had been called to do, and he was obedient to that calling. He knew he would be rewarded not only in his life on Earth, but in the afterlife. We have one life to live, and we must live it with passion and zeal. A life that is lived to love and serve others is a life that leaves its mark. That is how you will be remembered.

ACKNOWLEDGMENTS

I must give all honor and praise to my Lord and Savior, Jesus Christ, for without him I wouldn't have been able to write this book, let alone be alive today. I would also like to recognize the greatest joy and loves of my life—my kids, Reece, Elliot, Lane and Jordan. If it were not for them, I wouldn't be the dad I am today, which is my highest honor.

Many people have come into my life to inspire and model for me what love is. I want to recognize my Mom, who struggled to raise all six of us as a single parent and demonstrated courage every day; my brothers and sisters, who never gave up on me; my fiancé Amy, who stood by my side and helped me be the man I am today; my best friend Pat, who laid the grounds for me to become an author; and my first success coach Paula, who helped me believe anything is possible.

I have so many people who have mentored me and equipped me with the tools to succeed, such as Jack Canfield, Tony Robbins, Loren Lahov, Adrienne Duffy, Justin Breen, Mark Fujiwara and Nick Nanton. Every one of them has played a vital role in my development and growth as a person and a servant.

ADDITIONAL READING & RESOURCES

While writing this book, I referred to many others for guidance and many of the concepts ideas I found informed in the process. Some of the ideas in the books below also found their way into the text in one form another. As a supplement to this book, the most important and influential books I came across are listed below as additional reading.

———

Bolles, Richard N. *What Color Is Your Parachute? 2020: A Practical Manual for Job-Hunters and Career-Changers*. California: Ten Speed Press, 2019,

Holland, John, PhD. *Making Vocational Choices: A Theory of Vocational personalities and Work Environments*. Florida: Psychological Assessment Resources, 1997.

Kise, Jane A. G., David Stark, and Sandra Krebs Hirsh. LifeKeys: Discover Who You Are. Minnesota: Bethany House Publishing, 2005.

Rees, Erik. *S.H.A.P.E.: Finding and Fulfilling Your Unique Purpose for Life*. Michigan: Zondervan, 2006.

Robinson, Ken, PhD. *The Element: How Finding Your Passion Changes Everything*. New York: Penguin Books, 2008.

Robinson, Ken, PhD. *Finding your Element: How to Discover Your Talents and Passions and Transform Your Life*. New York: Penguin Books, 2013.

Tamashiro, Tim. *How to IKIGAI: lessons for finding happiness and living your life's purpose*. Mango publishing group 2019.

ABOUT THE AUTHOR

 Paul Peters is a bestselling author, motivational teacher and visionary entrepreneur. He is the owner and founder of Covenant Case Management Services, one of North Carolina's leading care providers for people with intellectual disabilities and those struggling with mental health and substance abuse issues. Peters is also the founder of the Nehemiah Project and International Foundation, faith-based non-profits serving at-risk children, seniors and veterans in North Carolina and Central America struggling with issues including domestic violence, addiction, homelessness and disabilities. He also hosts a TV show called *On Purpose with Paul*. Peters and his family live in Frisco, Texas.